AN ANTHOLOGY
OF GERMAN LITERATURE
OF THE ROMANTIC ERA AND
AGE OF GOETHE

AN ANTHOLOGY
OF GERMAN LITERATURE
OF THE ROMANTIC ERA AND
AGE OF GOETHE

Edited and Translated by

Klaus-Peter Hinze
and
Leonard M. Trawick

With Translations also by

Angela Elston, James Franklin,
Diana Hinze, and Sharon Richardson

EmText
San Francisco

Library of Congress Cataloging-in-Publication Data

An Anthology of German literature of the romantic era and age of
  Goethe / edited and translated by Klaus-Peter Hinze and Leonard M.
  Trawick ; with translations also by Angela Elston ... [et al.].
       p.   cm.
    English and German.
    ISBN 0-7734-1974-8
    1. German literature--18th century--Translations into English.
  2. German literature--19th century--Translations into English.
  I. Hinze, Klaus-Peter. II. Trawick, Leonard M.
  PT1113.A58 1993
  830.8'006--dc20   93-30394
                                                            CIP

Editorial Inquiries and Order Fulfillment:

The Edwin Mellen Press
P.O. Box 450
Lewiston, New York
14092 USA

Printed in the United States of America

TABLE OF CONTENTS

MAP OF GERMANY x

1: INTRODUCTION 1

2: GOTTFRIED AUGUST BÜRGER 11
    LENORE 12

3: JOHANN WOLFGANG VON GOETHE 31
    THE LITTLE HEATH ROSE 32
    MAY SONG 34
    PROMETHEUS 36
    THE ERLKING 40
    TO THE MOON 44
    THE HARPER 46
    MIGNON 48
    BLESSED YEARNING 50

4: FRIEDRICH SCHILLER 53
    THE GLOVE 54
    THE WALK 58
    ON NAIVE AND SENTIMENTAL POETRY 72

5: WILHELM HEINRICH WACKENRODER 81
    EFFUSIONS FROM THE HEART OF AN ART-LOVING MONK (EXCERPTS) 82

6: LUDWIG TIECK 91
    BLOND ECKBERT 92
    PUSS IN BOOTS 109

7: FRIEDRICH SCHLEGEL 171
    LYCEUM AND ATHENAEUM FRAGMENTS 172
    LONGING AND TRANQUILLITY 178

8: NOVALIS 181
    HYMNS TO THE NIGHT 182
    THE STORY OF HYACINTH AND ROSEBUD 194
    CHRISTENDOM, OR EUROPE 198

9: FRIEDRICH HÖLDERLIN 213
    TO THE FATES 214
    HYPERION'S SONG OF FATE 216

10: HEINRICH VON KLEIST 219
    ON THE MARIONETTE THEATER 220

11: JOSEPH VON EICHENDORFF 227
    THE TWO FRIENDS 228
    THE HERMIT 230

12: CLEMENS BRENTANO 233
    EVENING SERENADE 234
    THE SPINSTRESS'S SONG 236

13: HEINRICH HEINE 239
    THE LORELEI 240
    YOU ARE LIKE A FLOWER 242

The Rune Stone..242

A Fir Tree..244

Childe Harold 244

The Lotus Flower..246

From *The Romantic School*..248

14: Eduard Mörike..255

To a Lamp 256

To an Aeolian Harp..258

Appendix: German Romantic Philosophers......................261

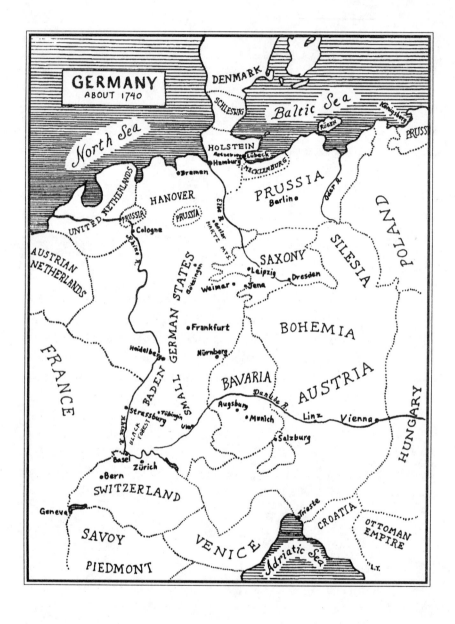

GERMANY
ABOUT 1740

DENMARK

SCHLESWIG

Baltic Sea

North Sea

HOLSTEIN

Lübeck

Hamburg

Bremen

MECKLENBURG

Rügen

Königsberg

PRUSS

UNITED NETHERLANDS

PRUSSIA

HANOVER

PRUSSIA

PRUSSIA

Berlin

Oder R.

POLAND

Cologne

Elbe R.

HARTZ MTS.

SAXONY

SILESIA

AUSTRIAN NETHERLANDS

Leipzig

Dresden

Göttingen

Weimar

Jena

Rhine R.

SMALL GERMAN STATES

Frankfurt

BOHEMIA

FRANCE

Heidelberg

Nürnberg

BADEN

BAVARIA

AUSTRIA

Strassburg

Tübingen

Ulm

Augsburg

Danube R.

Linz

Vienna

HUNGARY

Munich

BLACK FOREST

Salzburg

Basel

Zürich

Rhine R.

Bern

SWITZERLAND

Geneva

Trieste

CROATIA

OTTOMAN EMPIRE

SAVOY

VENICE

Adriatic Sea

PIEDMONT

I.T.

1

INTRODUCTION
THE ROMANTIC ERA IN GERMANY

German literary history divides the years 1770-1830 into three distinct periods: 1) Storm and Stress, 2) Classicism, and 3) Romanticism. But for the purposes of an international view of the literature of this period, it is useful to consider these sixty years all together as part of the Romantic Era in Europe. As has often happened, similar ideas, objectives, and goals sprang up at approximately the same time in several European countries, and influential literary works — expressions, perhaps, of a common *Zeitgeist,* such as Rousseau's *Nouvelle Héloïse,* MacPherson's Ossianic poems, and Goethe's *Sorrows of Young Werther* — left deep imprints in neighboring literatures as in their lands of origin. Indeed, in some ways the English Romantics were more akin to the German Storm and Stress writers and the older generations of poets — Goethe (1749-1832), Schiller (1759-1805), and Herder (1744-1803) — than to their Romantic contemporaries in Germany. From the viewpoint of the comparatist, it is justifiable to regard the youthful rebelliousness of the Storm and Stress period as Romantic or pre-Romantic; and similarly, Schiller's and Goethe's later ballads and fairy tales and the humanistic works of the Classical period can also legitimately be included in a discussion of Romantic literature.

In the late 1790s the German Romantics, properly so called, published their first significant works. This highly complex, varied, and often paradoxical cultural movement gave way to a new generation of writers around 1830. Although significant works continued to appear by Romantic latecomers such as Heinrich Heine (1797-1856) and Eduard Mörike (1804-1875), by the time of Goethe's death a more politically active generation, called Young Germany, assumed the literary vanguard. Nevertheless, the philosophy and aesthetic objectives of the Romantic school have remained alive and have had a continuing influence, for both good and ill, on the literary evolution of the past 170 years.

The years 1770-1830 were politically determined by the spirit of revolution abroad in the world. It was this epoch that saw the American War of Independence, the French Revolution, the Napoleonic wars with Europe's ensuing struggle for liberation, and the July Revolution of Paris. So it is only natural that the literary works of that time anticipate or mirror the political events and upheavals. The poets of Storm and Stress who gathered around Goethe and Herder in Strassburg, and young Schiller in Karlsruhe, were genuine revolutionaries, deeply committed to their political convictions. They demanded social justice and were united in their battle against despotism and absolutism. *"In tyrannos"* — let us fight against the tyrants! — the motto of Schiller's *Robbers,* could equally be that of his *Don Carlos* or Goethe's *Götz von Berlichingen* or even *Egmont.* They envisioned a better world where man's freedom and dignity were reality, not a dream. In later years, Goethe and Schiller assumed much more moderate political views and finally even came to the point where they strictly rejected the tactics of the French revolutionaries.

On the contrary, the younger generation of German Romantics proper, whose works appeared during the first three decades of the nineteenth century, were fundamentally unpolitical and fanatically private. Even though revolutionary in certain aspects of their moral-ethical value system, they remained basically reactionary in their refusal of political involvement. They lacked the commitment that the older writers had felt — a feeling for the cause of social and political improvement. There was much else, however, that the Romantics had inherited from the preceding era of Storm and Stress: a general spirit of iconoclasm and individualism, an interest in folk songs and tales, and a fascination with the culture, literature, architecture, and painting of the Middle Ages. Faced with the beauty of the Strassburg cathedral, Goethe felt a principle of construction comparable to that of an organic body and symbolic of the cultural unity of the Middle Ages. Most influential along these lines was Herder, who, following Bishop Percy in England, aroused new interest in folk songs, old ballads, and fairy tales.

Along with the revolutionary spirit exemplified in *Götz* and *The Robbers,* the Storm and Stress poets admired the exceptional man, the colossal personages of history and legend: Cain, Prometheus, Mohammed, Caesar, and — above all — Faust. This characteristic, which has earned Storm and Stress the epithet of the "genius movement," contributed to the intense individualism of the Romantics in the succeeding generation. Their most ardently admired hero was Shakespeare: "Nature! Nature! Nothing so completely Nature as Shakespeare's characters." Goethe, addressing Shakespeare, proclaims that, if he were still among the living, "I could not live anywhere else but with you!" Shakespeare's characters, language, rhythms, and dramatic structures became the models of poetic perfection.

The poets of Storm and Stress were ecstatic and rebellious; they were also, however, sentimental, melancholic, "sad unto death" to the same degree. Here another English influence is evident: the young poets were fascinated by the sentimentalism of Samuel Richardson's novels, and Thomas Gray's "Elegy Written in a Country Churchyard," the dark atmosphere of such works as Edward Young's *Night Thoughts,* and perhaps most of all by the archaism of James MacPherson's *Ossian* poems, with their tragic sense of fate and the unity of man and nature. It was this atmosphere that inspired young Goethe to the creation of his epistolary novel *The Sorrows of Young Werther,* which became an immediate success throughout the world upon its publication in 1774. Goethe's love and nature poetry written during this period, and influenced by the current interest in folk songs, ranks among the best of German lyric poetry. In the early seventies, Goethe also began his lifelong work on the story of Faust, which became of all German literature the most deeply and lastingly influential.

Following his assumption of responsibility as counsellor to the young Duke of Weimar in 1775, and his new interest in classical art stimulated by his reading of the classicist Johann Joachim Winckelmann (1717-1768) and his famous Italian Journey of 1786-88, Goethe renounced Storm and Stress and moved into what is called the period of Classicism. Schiller's thinking underwent a similar development, and German Classicism reached its height during the friendship of the two poets, from 1794 to Schiller's death in 1805. Perhaps a better word for German Classicism would be "Humanism": a keynote of Goethe's and Schiller's writings at this time is organic fulfillment of human potential, and integration of the individual with nature and society. While maintaining an Olympian view of history and a realization of mankind's repeated failure to live up to its ideals, the "Classical" attitude is typically one of calm hope that man can eventually achieve the harmonious existence of which he is capable, especially through the guidance of art. These qualities are exemplified by Schiller's "The Walk" (1797) and his *Wallenstein* trilogy (1800), and by Goethe's *Iphigenia in Tauris* (1787) and — in quite different veins — "The Fairy Tale" (1795) and the "education novel" *Wilhelm Meister's Apprenticeship* (1795-96). The last two works were especially popular with the Romantic writers, who tried to imitate and outdo the famous poet in these genres.

In 1798 Goethe and Schiller pursued intensive studies of the history and nature of the ballad, which they termed the "original egg" of all literary art since it fuses the three basic literary genres — narrative, drama, and lyric — into a unity. This year also saw the creation of some of their most beautiful ballads. At about the same time appeared the Gothic tale "Blond Eckbert" (1796) by Ludwig Tieck (1773-1853) and *Effusions from the Heart of an Art-Loving Monk* (1796-97) largely by his friend Wilhelm Heinrich Wackenroder (1773-1798). These are the first two works nowadays considered as true representatives of the new Romantic era. After Wackenroder's early death, Tieck joined a group of younger writers, who, in contrast to Goethe and Schiller, consciously saw themselves as a new breed of poets —Romantics. Here was August Wilhelm Schlegel (1767-1845), author of the outstanding Shakespeare translations; his brother

Friedrich (1772-1829), the theoretician of the new movement; the poet and mystic Novalis (Friedrich von Hardenberg, 1772-1801); together with the philosophers Johann Gottlieb Fichte (1762-1814) and Friedrich Schelling (1775-1854), who joined the group intermittently. We must not forget, as has been the case for almost two centuries, the women in these circles: especially Caroline von Schlegel, who translated major parts of the celebrated Shakespeare edition, and Dorothea Schlegel, daughter of Moses Mendelssohn and herself a writer of novels. They all constituted the core of the so-called Jena School or Early Romantics.

Another group of writers, the Later or Younger Romantics, assembled in Heidelberg. They were Clemens Brentano (1778-1842), Achim von Armin (1781-1831), and Josef von Görres (1776-1848), who collaborated on the first and foremost collection of folk songs, *Des Knaben Wunderhorn* (1806-08), and individually composed tales and lyrical poetry in the vein of folklore. They were joined for a time by the Silesian nobleman Joseph von Eichendorff (1788-1857), whose lyrical verses and novella, *Memoirs of a Good-for-Nothing,* have to our day been considered the most typical examples of Romanticism and have had a deep and far-reaching impact on German culture.

Too deeply individualistic to commit themselves to any of the literary schools, Friedrich Hölderlin (1770-1843) and Heinrich von Kleist (1777-1811) form a link between the pre-Romantic Goethe and Schiller and the Romantics proper. Their works — many Hellenistic in content, style, and structure — bear traces of both movements yet belong to neither.

Finally, in a third, more loosely connected group of Romantics, the Berlin School, may be included E.T.A. Hoffmann (1776-1822), a painter and musician as well as storyteller; Adalbert von Chamisso (1781-1838); and Friedrich von Fouque (1777-1843). From time to time, Arnim, Brentano, Adam Müller (1779-1829), Kleist, and Fichte stayed in Berlin, associated with this group, and were involved in its literary endeavors.

The brothers Jakob (1785-1863) and Wilhelm (1786-1859) Grimm pursued their work within the radius of Kassel, Marburg, and Göttingen, unearthing, writing, and editing the vastest collection of folk fairy tales, the richest source of primitive literary archetypes ever collected in Western culture. In the light of this achievement, it is easily forgotten that the brothers Grimm considered themselves primarily as philologists and linguists.

Special mention should be made of two authors who were latecomers to the Romantic School, though by no means epigones: the Swabian cleric Eduard Mörike and Heinrich Heine, journalist and lyricist of Jewish background, who spent the latter half of his life in Paris. Of particular fascination is the literary development Heine underwent, since his writing evolves from unmistakably Romantic lyric and prose to acidly analytic criticism.

A vast complex of new issues, ideas, and aesthetic tendencies, which can only be touched on here, contributes to the definition of the Romantic movement in Germany. The Romantics proper on the one hand felt themselves to be individualists, *poetae vates,* visionaries, cultural revolutionaries; on the other hand they searched for companionship. This explains the formation of several groups or schools within the movement and the close friendships between Romantic poets and their families that resulted more than once in marriages, divorces, and cross-marriages. Their characteristic, or even notorious, subjectivism, which exerted a tremendous influence on later generations of artists, and which was fostered by the philosophy of Immanuel Kant and his followers, especially Johann Gottlieb Fichte and Friedrich Schelling, led the Romantics to question ordinary assumptions as to what constitutes reality itself. Novalis rejects the clear, rational, but superficial light of day and sings "Hymns to the Night," the external darkness that permits internal illumination. In such tales as Hoffmann's "Golden Flower Pot" and Tieck's "Blond Eckbert" we are never allowed to be sure whether the supernatural events are to be taken as actual or as figments in the character's mind — and what standard can we have for the actual anyway, the authors imply, if all reality exists for us only in mental conceptions?

Romantic individualism also found expression in a love of the unbounded, the infinite, the unknown, the exotic, even the grotesque. Yet the longing for faraway regions, often noted as a predominant characteristic of German Romanticism — consider Goethe's "Mignon" songs and Novalis's fairy tales — proves to be a desire which can be fulfilled only at home.

These paradoxes occur in numerous guises; by glorifying antique art, for example, Hölderlin is finally led to believe in a cultural renaissance — in his own country. Their turning inward, away from external rules and forms, reinforced the Romantics' attraction to the naive, to the simple man and his art; and their interest in native German folklore became one of the most powerful springs of German nationalism.

The religious inclinations of the Romantics often led to mysticism, a search for unity with God or a mystical loved one, and thence back to an idealized pre-Reformation church. Some of these inclinations also find their expression in the forms of the dream and the fairy tale, literary types which convey effectively the merging of the here-and-now with the realms of imagination. The immense number of fairy tales written by the Romantics testifies to their *Angst,* their desperate flight from bourgeois demands, their fear of a commitment that would tie them to the limiting existence of respectable citizenry. Here was offered to them another path back into the security afforded only by their inner selves.

Romantic subjectivity reaches an almost pathological extreme in the literary phenomenon generally called Romantic irony. This term describes an aesthetic self-consciousness in which the writer explores and analyzes his creative processes simultaneously with the writing of his work, so that the two levels of expression neutralize each other. Romantic irony can take the subtle form of slight exaggeration, as for example in Heine's "Lotus Flower," where the poet uses just one decorative adjective too many, thereby undermining his own creation, yet accepting, or even admiring it. Or the technique can be used to the farcical extremes exhibited in Tieck's *Puss in Boots.* At its best, Romantic irony transcends the destructive self-consciousness which Kleist so neatly describes in "On the Marionette Theater." The artist's ever-present critical "I" follows the creative process within himself, thus establishing between the creator and his creation an aesthetic distance that makes conscious evaluation an integral part of the artistic activity. The artist's consciousness thus lingers in the realm between his own most personal imagination and the outside world, society, and nature. By appointing himself his own judge, the Romantic writer precludes outside intervention, retreating to where he holds dialogue with himself only. This attitude, which has been carried to a climax by the twentieth-century writers of the *nouveau roman,* the theater of the absurd, and such novelists as Thomas Mann, the "ironic German" — has its roots in the agonizing conflict between the creative inner self and outer reality, a conflict that notably engaged the Romantic poets. Although it was at first largely a German phenomenon (with traces in a few English works such as Laurence Sterne's *Tristram Shandy* and Byron's *Don Juan*), by the end of the nineteenth century the writer's alienation from his own work had become a widespread attitude and technique. This is only one of the many strains now deeply ingrained in modern literature that readers will discover in the selections in this book, along with much that is of permanent literary value for its own sake.

When we decided on this selection we were guided by very practical criteria. We included as many first-rate, typical, and influential works as possible, but left out those that are readily available in inexpensive editions. Thus some poetry by Goethe is included, but his *Young Werther, Faust,* and "Fairy Tale" are omitted. For the same reason E.T.A. Hoffmann's tales and Kleist's novellas and dramas were left out. We would have liked to include many more literary works, and indeed German Romantic paintings, music, and landscape architecture as well. But we hope this selection will provide at least a beginning for further studies in German — or better, European and American — Romanticism.

A NOTE ON THE TRANSLATIONS

The translations are by Leonard Trawick in consultation with Klaus-Peter Hinze, with the following exceptions: selections from Friedrich Schlegel are translated by Sharon Richardson; selections from Wackenroder partly by Angela Elston; *Puss in Boots* largely by James Franklin; Novalis's "Story of Hyacinth and Rosebud" and Kleist's "On the Marionette Theater" by Angela Elston; and excerpts from Heine's *The Romantic School* by Diana Hinze.

An attempt has been made to reproduce the metrical form of the verse selections, but in a few cases, notably Goethe's lyrics, the original rhyme scheme could not be followed without excessive distortion. Because poetry inevitably loses more than prose in translation, especially the effects of sound, the German originals are provided alongside the English versions.

ઠ⁊

2

GOTTFRIED AUGUST BÜRGER
(1747-1794)

Bürger was the author of ballads, translator of Homer and Shakespeare, and a well-known editor. His most popular work was *Lenore* (1773), which soon had a number of English translators, including Sir Walter Scott, whose version was called "William and Helen" (1796).

LENORE

Lenore fuhr ums Morgenrot
Empor aus schweren Träumen
"Bist untreu, Wilhelm, oder tot?
Wie lange willst du säumen?" —
Er war mit König Friedrichs Macht
Gezogen in die Prager Schlacht
Und hatte nicht geschrieben,
Ob er gesund geblieben.

Der König und die Kaiserin,
Des langen Haders müde,
Erweichten ihren harten Sinn
Und machten endlich Friede;
Und jedes Heer, mit Sing und Sang,
Mit Paukenschlag und Kling und Klang,
Geschmückt mit grünen Reisern,
Zog heim zu seinen Häusern.

Und überall, allüberall,
Auf Wegen und auf Stegen,
Zog alt und jung dem Jubelschall
Der Kommenden entgegen.
"Gottob!" rief Kind und Gattin laut,
"Wilkommen!" manche frohe Braut.
Ach! aber für Lenoren
War Gruss und Kuss verloren.

Sie frug den Zug wohl auf und ab
Und frug nach allen Namen;
Doch keiner war, der Kundschaft gab,
Von allen, so da kamen.
Als nun das Heer vorüber war,

LENORE

Lenore rose up from heavy dreams
With the first red gleam of day—
"Oh, William, are you false—or dead?
How long will you delay?"
Since he had joined King Frederick's men
And marched to fight at Prague, there'd been
No letter home to tell
If he were safe and well.

The King and Empress, tired, agreed
Their quarreling should cease,
And, softening their hearts at last,
They made a pact of peace.
Both armies then, with cheers and singing,
And drums and pipes and rattle and ringing,
Bedecked with garlands gay,
Homeward made their way.

And everywhere the young and old
All hurried out to meet
The returning soldiers' joyous noise
On every road and street.
"Thank God!" the wives and children cried,
And, "Welcome!" murmured many a bride:
But for Lenore, alas,
There was no greeting kiss.

Asking, she went along the ranks—
Asking for every name:
No word of William could she glean
From all the men who came.
When all the troops had passed her there

Zerraufte sie ihr Rabenhaar
Und warf sich hin zur Erde
Mit wütiger Gebärde.

Die Mutter lief wohl hin zu ihr:
"Ach, dass sich Gott erbarme!
Du trautes Kind, was ist mit dir?"
Und schloss sie in die Arme. —
"O Mutter, Mutter! Hin ist hin!
Nun fahre Welt und alles hin!
Bei Gott ist kein Erbarmen;
O weh, o weh mir Armen!"

"Hilf Gott, hilf! Sieh uns gnädig an!
Kind, bet ein Vaterunser!
Was Gott tut, das ist wohlgetan.
Gott, Gott erbarmt sich unser!"
"O Mutter, Mutter! eitler Wahn!
Gott hat an mir nicht wohl getan!
Was half, was half mein Beten?
Nun ist's nicht mehr von nöten."

"Hilf Gott, hilf! Wer den Vater kennt,
Der weiss, er hilft den Kindern.
Das hochgelobte Sakrament
Wird deinen Jammer lindern."
"O Mutter, Muter, was mich brennt,
Das lindert mir kein Sakrament!
Kein Sakrament mag Legen
Den Toten wiedergeben."

"Hör, Kind! Wie, wenn der falsche Mann
Im fernen Ungarlande
Sich seines Glaubens abgetan

She shrieked and tore her raven hair,
And flinging herself down,
Thrashed wildly on the ground.

Her anxious mother ran to her:
"God shelter us from harms!
What ails you, dearest child?" she cried,
And took her in her arms.
"Oh Mother, what is done is done!
My world, my everything is gone!
God has abandoned me!
Oh woe, oh misery!"

"Help, God, oh help us in our need!
My child, kneel down and pray!
What God has done is for the best.
God, pity us this day!"
"Oh mother, vain credulity!
God has not done the best for me.
What help was all my praying?
No prayer is now worth saying."

"God help us! Those who know the Lord
Know how He helps His own;
The holy sacrament will ease
What makes you grieve and moan."
"Oh mother, that which burns my breast
No sacrament can lay to rest.
No sacrament can bring
The dead to life again."

"Listen, my child, what if that man
Was false, and what if he
Renounced his faith to win a bride

Zum neuen Ehebande?
Lass fahren, Kind, sein Herz dahin!
Er hat es nimmermehr Gewinn!
Wann Seel' und Leib sich trennen,
Wird ihn sein Meineid brennen."

"O Mutter, Mutter, hin ist hin!
Verloren ist verloren!
Der Tod, der Tod ist mein Gewinn!
O wär' ich nie geboren!
Lisch aus, mein Licht, auf ewig aus!
Stirb hin, stirb hin in Nacht und Graus!
Bei Gott ist kein Erbarmen;
O weh, o weh mir Armen!"

"Hilf Gott, hilf! Geh nicht ins Gericht
Mit deinem armen Kinde!
Sie weiss nicht, was die Zunge spricht;
Behalt ihr nicht die Sünde!
Ach, Kind, vergiss dien irdisch Leid
Und denk an Gott und Seligkeit,
So wird doch deiner Seelen
Der Bräutigam nicht fehlen." —

"O Mutter! was ist Seligkeit?
O Mutter! was ist Hölle?
Bei ihm, bei ihm ist Seligkeit
Und ohne Wilhelm Hölle! —
Lisch aus, mein Licht, auf ewig aus!
Stirb hin, stirb hin in Nacht und Graus!
Ohn' ihn mag ich auf Erden,
Mag dort nicht selig werden." —

In far-off Hungary?
No profit comes from such a heart;
So freely, child, let it depart:
When soul from body's free,
He'll burn for treachery."

"Oh Mother, what is done is done!
And what is gone is gone!
Death is my profit, only death!
Would I were never born!
Go out, forever out, my light—
Die, die in horror and in night!
God has abandoned me!
Oh woe, oh misery!"

"Help, God, oh help! And judge not ill
Thy wretched erring child;
She knows not what her tongue has said,
These sinful words and wild!
Oh child, forget your earthly grief;
To God and Heaven turn your belief;
Your soul will find above
Its bridegroom and true love."

"Oh Mother, what to me is Heaven?
Oh Mother, what is Hell?
With William only is my Heaven,
Without him is my Hell!
Go out, forever out, my light—
Die, die in horror and in night!
Above or here below,
Without him all is woe."

So wütete Verzweifelung
Ihr in Gehirn und Adern.
Sie fuhr mit Gottes Vorsehung
Vermessen fort zu hadern,
Zerschlug den Busen und zerrang
Die Hand bis Sonnenuntergang,
Bis auf am Himmelsbogen
Die goldnen Sterne zogen.

Und aussen, horch! ging's trapp trapp trapp
Als wie von Rosseshufen,
Und klirrend stieg ein Reiter ab
An des Geländers Stufen.
Und horch! und horch den Pfortenring,
Ganz lose, leise, klinglingling!
Dann kamen durch die Pforte
Vernehmlich diese Worte:

"Holla, holla! Tu auf, mein Kind!
Schläfst, Liebchen, oder wachst du?
Wie bist noch gegen mich gesinnt?
Und weinest oder lachst du?"
"Ach, Wilhelm, du?.. So spät bei Nacht?
Geweinet hab' ich und gewacht;
Ach, grosses Leid erlitten!
Wo kommst du hergeritten?" —

"Wir satteln nur um Mitternacht.
Weit ritt ich her von Böhmen.
Ich habe spät mich aufgemacht
Und will dich mit mir nehmen."
"Ach, Wilhelm, erst herein geschwind!
Den Hagedorn durchsaust der Wind,
Herein, in meinen Armen,
Herzliebster, zu erwarmen!" —

And thus the madness of despair
Raged through her brain and blood.
She railed in rash protest against
The providence of God.
She wrung her hands, she beat her breast,
Until the sun sank to its rest,
And into heaven's dome
The golden stars had come.

Then outside—hark! A *trapp, trapp, trapp,*
Like horses' hooves, resounded;
Then—jingling at the lower step:
A rider had dismounted.
And—what was that? The old loose ring
That held the gate went *kling ling ling;*
And through the gate there came
A voice, distinct and plain;

"Hallo! My darling, open up!
Are you awake or sleep?
How do you feel about me, girl—
And do you laugh or weep?"
"Oh, William—you? At night? So late?
How I have wept and lain awake,
With grief quite overcome!
—Where have you ridden from?"

"We saddle only late at night;
I've ridden all the way
From far Bohemia so late
To carry you away."
"First, William, quick, in here with me!
The wind blows through the hawthorn tree;
Come in, into my arms.
Love, let me make you warm!"

"Lass sausen durch den Hagedorn,
Lass sausen, Kind, lass sausen!
Der Rappe scharrt; es klirrt der Sporn.
Ich darf allhier nicht hausen.
Komm, schürze, spring und schwinge dich
Auf meinen Rappen hinter mich!
Muss heut noch hundert Meilen
Mit dir ins Brautbett eilen."

"Ach, wolltest hundert Meilen noch
Mich heut ins Brautbett tragen?
Und horch! es brummt die Glocke noch,
Die elf schon angeschlagen. —
"Sieh hin, sieh her! der Mond scheint hell.
Wir und die Toten reiten schnell.
Ich bringe dich, zur Wette,
Noch heut ins Hochzeitbette."

"Sag an, wo ist dein Kämmerlein?
Wo? wie dein Hochzeitbettchen?"
"Weit, weit von hier!..Still, kühl und klein!..
Sechs Bretter und zwei Brettchen!"
"Hat's Raum für mich?" — "Für dich und mich!
Komm, schürze, spring und schwinge dich!
Die Hochzeitgäste hoffen;
Die Kammer steht uns offen."

Schön Liebchen schürzte, sprang und schwang
Sich auf das Ross behende;
Wohl um den trauten Reiter schlang
Sie ihre Lilienhände;
Und hurre hurre, hopp hopp hopp!
Ging's fort in sausendem Galopp,

"Let the wind blow through the hawthorne tree,
Let it blow, girl, let it blow!
My black steed stamps, my spurs ring shrill,
And we have far to go!
Come, tuck your skirts, jump up in back,
Behind me on my pawing Black!
There's a hundred miles ahead,
Before our bridal bed!"

"What! ride a hundred miles tonight
To find my bridal bower?
Listen! The clock already sounds!
It is the eleventh hour."
"There's no two ways: the moon shines bright.
We and the dead ride fast tonight.
Before the dawn gleams red,
You'll find your bridal bed."

"But say, where is your little room?
Where do you sleep?" she said.
"Far, far from here . . . quiet, cool, and small.
Six planks—two boards, the bed."
"There's room for me?" "For you and me!
Come, tuck your skirts, climb on and see;
The guests await the bride,
The room stands open wide."

The pretty dear tucked up her skirt,
Jumped on the horse behind him;
And to hold the darling horseman tight,
Her lily hands entwined him.
Then — hup, hup, hup! hi-o, hi-o!
The gasping horse and rider go

Das Ross und Reiter schnoben,
Und Kies und Funken stoben.

Zur rechten und sur linken Hand
Vorbei vor ihren Blicken,
Wie flogen Anger, Heid' und Land!
Wie donnerten die Brücken!
"Graut Liebchen auch?.. Der Mond scheint hell!
Hurra! Die Toten reiten schnell!
Graut Liebchen auch vor Toten?"
"Ach nein!...Doch lass die Toten!"

Was klang dort für Gesang und Klang
Was flatterten die Raben?...
Horch Glockenklang! Horch Totensang:
"Lasst uns den Leib begraben!"
Und näher zog ein Leichenzug,
Der Sarg und Totenbahre trug.
Das Lied war zu vergleichen
Dem Unkenruf in Teichen.

"Nach Mitternacht begrabt den Leib
Mit Klang und Sang und Klage!
Jetzt führ' ich heim mein junges Weib;
Mit, mit zum Brautgelage!
Komm, Küster, hier! komm mit dem Chor
Und gurgle mir das Brautlied vor!
Komm, Pfaff', und sprich den Segen,
Eh' wir zu Bett uns legen!"

Still Klang und Sang.. Die Bahre schwand..
Gehorsam seinem Rufen
Kam's hurre hurre! nachgerannt
Hart hinter's Rappen Hufen.

At such a headlong clatter,
The sparks and pebbles scatter.

On right and left they seem to cleave
The whirling land asunder!
Past field and common, heath and green—
And how the bridges thunder!
"Afraid, my dear? . . . The moon shines bright!
Hurrah! The dead ride fast tonight!
Does dearie fear the dead?"
"No . . . but, forget the dead!"

What song and music did they hear?
Why were those ravens flurried?
 Hark—bells! And hark—a funeral choir:
"Come, let the dead be buried!"
A funeral train was passing near
Bearing the coffin and the bier;
The chant seemed dismal, broken,
Like frogs in ditches croaking.

"Postpone your chants and burial—
Till late tonight at least!
I'm bringing home my sweetheart now—
Come, join the wedding feast!
Come, sexton—priest, choir—come along,
And croak for me the bridal song!
A blessing must be said
Before we lie in bed!"

Bier vanished . . . music, chant were stilled . . .
Obedient to his call,
Hup, hup! Behind Black's hooves they came,
Priest, sexton, choir and all:

Und immer weiter, hopp hopp hopp!
Ging's fort in sausendem Galopp,
Dass Ross und Reiter schnoben
Und Kies und Funken stoben.

Wie flogen rechts, wie flogen links
Gebirge, Bäum' und Hecken!
Wie flogen links und rechts und links
Die Dörfer, Städt' und Flecken! —
"Graut Liebchen auch?.. Der Mond scheint hell!
Hurra! Die Toten reiten schnell!
Graut Liebchen auch vor Toten?
"Ach! Lass sie ruhn, die Toten." —

Sieh da! sieh da! Am Hochgericht
Tanzt' um des Rades Spindel,
Halb sichtbarlich bei Mondenlicht,
Ein laftiges Gesindel.
"Sa sa! Gesindel, hier! komm hier!
Gesindel komm und folge mir!
Tanz uns den Hochzeitreigen,
Wann wir zu Bette steigen!"

Und das Gesindel, husch husch husch!
Kam hinten nachgeprasselt,
Wie Wirbelwind am Haselbusch
Durch dürre Blätter rasselt.
Und weiter, weiter, hopp hopp hopp!
Ging's fort in sausendem Galopp,
Dass Ross und Reiter schnoben
Und Kies und Funken stoben.

And onward still, hi-o, hi-o!
The gasping horse and rider go
At such a headlong clatter,
The sparks and pebbles scatter.

Past on the right, past on the left
Flew hedges, trees, and hills;
And past them left and right and left
Flew hamlets, towns, and mills.
Afraid, my dear? . . . The moon shines bright!
Hurrah! The dead ride fast tonight!
Does dearie fear the dead?"
"Oh, let them rest, the dead."

Look there! Look there! Round a gallows-tree
Like a wheel around an axle,
Half visible in the pale moonlight,
There danced a ghostly rabble.
"Hoy there, you rabble, come away
And dance our marriage roundelay
When my dear and I are wed
And climb into our bed!"

The rabble followed close behind
With raucous, whispering bustle,
Like fitful wind in a hazel bush,
That makes the dry leaves rustle.
Then onward, hup! Hi-o, hi-o!
The gasping horse and rider go
At such a headlong clatter,
The sparks and pebbles scatter.

Wie flog, was rund der Mond beschien,
Wie flog es in die Ferne!
Wie flogen oben überhin
Der Himmel und die Sterne! —
"Graut Liebchen auch?.. Der Mond scheint hell!
Hurra! Die Toten reiten schnell! —
Graut Liebchen auch vor Toten?" —
"O weh! Lass ruhn die Toten!"

"Rapp'! Rapp'! mich dünkt, der Hahn schon ruft..
Bald wird der Sand verrinnen..
Rapp'! Rapp'! ich wittre Morgenluft..
Rapp'! tummle dich von hinnen!
Vollbracht, vollbracht ist unser Lauf!
Das Hochzeitbette tut sich auf!
Die Toten reiten schnelle!
Wir sind, wir sind zur Stelle."

Rasch auf ein eisern Gittertor
Ging's mit verhängtem Zügel;
Mit schwanker Gert' ein Schlag davor
Zersprengte Schloss und Riegel.
Die Flügel flogen klirrend auf,
Und über Gräber ging der Lauf.
Es blinkten Leichensteine
Rundum im Mondenscheine.

Ha sieh! Ha sieh! Im Augenblick,
Huhu! ein grässlich Wunder!
Des Reiters Koller, Stück für Stück,
Fiel ab wie mürber Zunder.
Zum Schädel ohne Zopf und Schopf,
Zum nackten Schädel ward sein Kopf,
Sein Körper zum Gerippe
Mit Stundenglas und Hippe.

How it all flew past, left far behind—
How the moonlit scenes flew by!
And how, far up above their heads,
Flew past the stars and sky!
"Afraid, my dear? The moon shines bright!
Hurrah! The dead ride fast tonight!
Does dearie fear the dead?"
"Ah, leave in peace the dead!"

On Black! On Black! The sands run out!
Is that a cock I hear?
On Black! I whiff the morning air!
On Black! Away from here!
It's done, it's done—our fearful ride!
The marriage bed welcomes the bride!
Ha, ha! The dead ride fast!
We've reached the place at last!

Directly towards an iron-barred gate
With loose-held reins they thunder—
He swings his limber switch and bursts
The lock and bolt asunder:
The gates clang open, and inside
Right over rows of graves they ride,
Around them every tomb
Gleaming beneath the moon.

Oh, look! Oh look! Quick as a wink
Oh, ugh! A gruesome wonder!
The horseman's jacket, piece by piece,
Fell off like rotten tinder.
His head became a death's head bare,
Without a scalp or lock of hair;
He was a skeleton,
Hourglass and scythe and bone!

Hoch bäumte sich, wild schnob der Rapp'
Und sprühte Feuerfunken;
Und hui! war's unter ihr hinab
Verschwunden und versunken.
Geheul! Geheul aus hoher Luft,
Gewinsel kam aus tiefer Gruft.
Lenorens Herz mit Beben
Rang zwischen Tod und Leben.

Nun tanzten wohl bei Mondenglanz
Rundum herum im Kreise
Die Geister einen Kettentanz
Und heulten diese Weise:
"Geduld! Geduld! Wenn's Herz auch bricht!
Mit Gott im Himmel hadre nicht!
Des Leibes bist du ledig;
Gott sei der Seele gnädig!"

The snorting, rearing, wild black horse
Flung fire-sparks all around;
Then—hey! beneath Lenore he sank
And vanished in the ground.
Then, howls! Howls rent the upper air,
And from the graves, groans of despair.
Her heart quaked at the strife,
Torn between Death and Life.

And now indeed the spirits danced
Around her in a ring,
Linked in a chain, beneath the moon
With shrieks and howls they sing:
"Have patience though your heart be riven;
Never contend with God in Heaven.
From earth you have release—
God grant your soul His peace."

3

JOHANN WOLFGANG VON GOETHE
(1749-1832)

Generally considered Germany's greatest poet, Goethe wrote a number
of influential plays (*Götz von Berlichingen,* 1773; *Iphigenia in Tauris,*
1787; and *Egmont,* 1788); novels (*The Sorrows of Young Werther,* 1774;
Wilhelm Meister's Apprenticeship, 1796); and the great poetic drama *Faust*
(Part I, 1808; Part II, 1832). His many lyric poems, which are represented
here, were also highly influential. They often reflect Goethe's interest in
folk songs (some, such as "The Little Heath Rose," are actually adaptations
of existing songs. "Mignon" and "The Harper" originally appeared as part
of *Wilhelm Meister's Apprenticeship;* "Mignon" exemplifies the love of
Italy and Greece common in German literature of this period.

HEIDENRÖSLEIN

Sah ein Knab ein Röslein stehn,
Röslein auf der Heiden,
War so jung und morgenschön,
Lief er schnell, es nah zu sehn,
Sah's mit vielen Freuden.
Röslein, Röslein, Röslein rot,
Röslein auf der Heiden.

Knabe sprach: Ich breche dich,
Röslein auf der Heiden!
Röslein sprach: Ich steche dich,
Dass du ewig denkst an mich,
Und ich will's nicht leiden.
Röslein, Röslein, Röslein rot,
Röslein auf der Heiden.

Und der wilde Knabe brach
's Röslein auf der Heiden;
Röslein wehrte sich und stach,
Half ihm doch kein Weh und Ach,
Musst' es eben leiden.
Röslein, Röslein, Röslein rot,
Röslein auf der Heiden.

THE LITTLE HEATH ROSE

A boy saw a little rose in bloom.
Little rose on the heath;
She was so young, fair as the dawn;
He ran to see her closely—
She filled his heart with joy.
Rose, rose, little red rose,
Little rose on the heath.

Boy said: I shall pick you,
Little rose on the heath.
Rose answered, no, I'll prick you
So deep you'll not forget me—
I'll never, never let you.
Rose, rose, little red rose,
Little rose on the heath.

The wanton boy did pick
The little rose on the heath.
She fought and stabbed him with her thorn,
But all her cries and tears were vain,
She simply had to let him.
Rose, rose, little red rose,
Little rose on the heath.

MAILIED

Wie herrlich leuchtet
Mir die Natur!
Wie glänzt die Sonne!
Wie lacht die Flur!

Es dringen Blüten
Aus jedem Zweig
Und tausend Stimmen
Aus dem Gesträuch

Und Freud' und Wonne
Aus jeder Brust.
O Erd', o Sonne!
O Glück, o Lust!

O Lieb', o Liebe!
So golden schön,
Wie Morgenwolken
Auf jenen Höhn!

Du segnest herrlich
Das frische Feld,
Im Blütendampfe
Die volle Welt.

O Mädchen, Mädchen,
Wie lieb' ich dich!
Wie blickt dein Auge!
Wie liebst du mich!

So liebt die Lerche
Gesang und Luft,

MAY SONG

Nature sparkles
With such splendor!
Sunshine glitters,
Fields rejoice!

Blossoms burst
From every branch,
A thousand songs
From every bush,

Delight and bliss
From every heart.
Oh Earth, oh sun!
Oh mirth, oh joy!

Oh love, oh love,
So fair and bright,
Like morning clouds
That crown those hills—

Your radiance blesses
The dewy field,
In blossom-mist
The whole wide world!

Dear girl, dear girl,
How I love you!
How your eyes shine
With love for me!

Just as the lark
Loves song and air,

Und Morgenblumen
Den Himmelsduft,

Wie ich dich liebe
Mit warmem Blut,
Die du mir Jugend
Und Freud und Mut

Zu neuen Liedern
Und Tanzen gibst
Sei ewig glücklich,
Wie du mich liebst!

PROMETHEUS

Bedecke deinen Himmel, Zeus,
Mit Wolkendunst
Und übe, dem Knaben gleich,
Der Disteln köpft,
An Eichen dich und Bergeshöhn;
Musst mir meine Erde
Doch lassen stehn
Und meine Hütte, die du nicht gebaut,
Und meinen Herd,
Um dessen Glut
Du mich beneidest.

And morning blossoms
The fragrant sky,

So my blood warms
With love for you
Who give me youth
And joy and heart

To dance and sing
As never before!
Be ever happy
In your love for me!

PROMETHEUS

Cover your heavens, Zeus,
With cloudy mist
And practice, like a boy
Beheading thistles,
On oaks and mountain tops;
But you must leave me
My earth still standing,
And my cottage, which you did not build,
And my hearth
Whose glow
You envy me.

Ich kenne nichts Ärmeres
Unter der Sonn' als euch, Götter!
Ihr nähret kümmerlich
Von Opfersteuern
Und Gebetshauch
Eure Majestät
Und darbtet, wären
Nicht Kinder und Bettler
Hoffnungsvolle Toren.

Da ich ein Kind war,
Nicht wusste, wo aus noch ein,
Kehrt ich mein verirrtes Auge
Zur Sonne, als wenn drüber wär'
Ein Ohr, zu hören meine Klage,
Ein Herz wie meins,
Sich des Bedrängten zu erbarmen.

Wer half mir
Wider der Titanen Übermut?
Wer rettete vom Tode mich,
Von Sklaverei?
Hast du nicht alles selbst vollendet,
Heilig glühend Herz?
Und glühtest jung und gut,
Betrogen, Rettungsdank
Dem Schlafenden da droben?

Ich dich ehren? Wofür?
Hast du die Schmerzen gelindert
Je des Beladenen?
Hast du dieTränen gestillet
Je des Geängsteten?
Hat nicht mich zum Manne geschmiedet

I know nothing poorer
Under the sun than you gods!
Wretchedly you nourish
Your majesty
On sacrifices
And the breath of prayers,
And you would starve
If children and beggars
Were not hopeful fools.

When I was a child,
Not knowing which way to turn,
I raised my bewildered eyes
To the sun, as if up above
Was an ear to hear my lament,
A heart like mine
To pity the afflicted.

Who helped me
Against the Titans' insolence?
Who rescued me from death,
From slavery?
Did you not do all this yourself,
My staunch and sacred heart?
And did you not, young and good, deceived,
Glow with thanks for rescue
To one who was sleeping above?

I honor you? For what?
Have you ever eased the suffering
Of those who were heavy laden?
Have you ever dried the tears
Of the frightened?
Was I not forged into a man

Die allmächtige Zeit
Und das ewige Schicksal,
Meine Herren und deine?

Wähntest du etwa,
Ich sollte das Leben hassen,
In Wüsten fliehen,
Weil nicht alle
Blütenträume reiften?

Hier sitz ich, forme Menschen
Nach meinem Bilde,
Ein Geschlecht,
das mir gleich sei,
Zu leiden, zu weinen,
Zu geniessen und zu freuen sich,
Und dein nicht zu achten,
Wie ich!

ERLKÖNIG

Wer reitet so spät durch Nacht und Wind?
Es ist der Vater mit seinem Kind;
Er hat den Knaben wohl in dem Arm,
Er fasst ihn sicher, er hält ihn warm.

"Mein Sohn, was birgst du so bang dein Gesicht?"—
Siehst, Vater, du den Erlkönig nicht?

By almighty Time
And eternal Fate,
My masters and yours?

Did you fancy
That I should hate life
And flee into the deserts
Because not all
My blossom dreams ripened?

Here I sit, forming men
In my own image,
A race to be like me,
To suffer, to weep,
To delight and to rejoice,
And to ignore you,
As I do.

THE ERLKING

Who rides so late through the night so wild?
It is a father with his child;
He holds the boy fast in his arm,
He grips him tightly, he keeps him warm.

"My son, why hide your face in fear?"
Don't you see, Father, the Erlking near?

Den Erlenkönig mit Kron' und Schweif?—
"Mein Sohn, es ist ein Nebelstreif."
"Du liebes Kind, komm, geh mit mir!
Gar schöne Spiele spiel' ich mit dir;
Manch' bunte Blumen sind an dem Strand,
Meine Mutter hat manch gülden Gewand."

Mein Vater, mein Vater, und hörest du nicht,
Was Erlenkönig mir leise verspricht?—
"Sei ruhig, bleibe ruhig, mein Kind;
In dürren Blättern säuselt der Wind."

"Willst, feiner Knabe, du mit mir gehn?
Meine Töchter sollen dich warten schön;
Meine Töchter führen den nächtlichen Reihn,
Und wiegen und tanzen und singen dich ein."

Mein Vater, mein Vater, und siehst du nicht dort
Erlkönigs Töchter am düstern Ort?—
"Mein Sohn, mein Sohn, ich seh' es genau:
Es scheinen die alten Weiden so grau."

"Ich liebe dich, mich reizt deine schöne Gestalt;
Und bist du nicht willig, so brauch' ich Gewalt."—
Mein Vater, mein Vater, jetzt fasst er mich an!
Erlkönig hat mir ein Leids getan!—

Dem Vater grauset's, er reitet geschwind,
Er hält in Armen das ächzende Kind,
Erreicht den Hof mit Müh' und Not;
In seinen Armen das Kind war tot.

The Erlking, with his crown and tail?
"My son, that's fog down in the vale."

"You darling child, come go with me,
I've lovely games to play with thee!
Many bright flowers are growing there,
And my mother has golden clothes to wear."

O Father, oh Father, can't you hear
The Erlking whispering promises near?
"Be calm, my child, oh, rest at ease,
The wind's just rustling through the trees.

"Pretty boy, won't you go with me there?
My daughters will give you lovely care—
At night they'll dance with you in a ring,
And they'll rock you to sleep and sweetly sing."

Oh Father, oh Father, now can't you see
The Erlking's daughters by that dark tree?
"Dear son, dear son, I see it clear—
Some old gray willows by the weir."

"I love you, your beauty makes my blood course!
Come willingly, dear, or I'll take you by force."
Oh Father, he's clutching with all his might,
The Erlking hurts me, he holds so tight!

The terrified father rides onward apace,
With the groaning child in his anxious embrace;
He reaches the court-yard exhausted with dread,
But in his arms the child was dead.

AN DEN MOND

Füllest wieder Busch und Tal
Still mit Nebelglanz,
Lösest endlich auch einmal
Meine Seele ganz;

Breitest über mein Gefild
Lindernd deinen Blick,
Wie des Freundes Auge mild
Über mein Geschick.

Jeden Nachklang fühlt mein Herz
Froh' und trüber Zeit,
Wandle zwischen Freud' und Schmerz
In der Einsamkeit.

Fliesse, fliesse, lieber Fluss!
Nimmer werd' ich froh!
So verrauschte Scherz und Kuss,
Und die Treue so.

Ich besass es doch einmal,
Was so köstlich ist!
Dass man doch zu seiner Qual
Nimmer es vergisst!

Rausche, Fluss, das Tal entlang,
Ohne Rast und Ruh,
Rausche, flüstre meinem Sang
Melodien zu!

TO THE MOON

Once more you fill valley and glade
With silent, misty splendor,
And again, at last, set free
My whole spirit.

Over these fields you cast
Your soothing regard,
Like a friend's gentle eye
Over my fate.

My heart feels every echo
Of happy times and sad;
I wander between joy and pain,
In solitude.

Flow on, flow on, dear river!
I'll never find happiness!
Mirth and kisses, like you, have flowed away,
And good faith too.

Yet I had it once—
What is so precious!
And ah, the torment is—
It is never forgotten!

Rush on, river, down the valley,
Without rest or peace;
Murmur, whisper the music
Of my song,

Wenn du in der Winternacht
Wütend überschwillst,
Oder um die Frühlingspracht
Junger Knospen quillst.

Selig, wer sich vor der Welt
Ohne Hass verschliesst,
Einen Freund am Busen hält
Und mit dem geniesst,

Was, von Menschen nicht gewusst,
Oder nicht bedacht,
Durch das Labyrinth der Brust
Wandelt in der Nacht.

From *Wilhelm Meister's Apprenticeship* (*Wilhelm Meisters Lehrjahre*)

HARFENSPIELER

Wer nie sein Brot mit Tränen ass,
Wer nie die kummervollen Nächte
Auf seinem Bette einend sass,
Der kennt euch nicht, ihr himlischen Mächte.

Ihr führt ins Leben uns hinein,
Ihr lasst den Armen schuldig werden,
Dann überlasst ihr ihn der Pein:
Denn alle Schuld rächt sich auf Erden.

Whether in the winter night
You rage and overflow,
Or gush among the spring glory
Of young buds.

Happy is he who without hate
Retires from the world,
Clasping a friend to his bosom
With whom to savor

That which—unknown to the world
Or never thought of—
Through the labyrinth of the heart
Wanders in the night.

From *Wilhelm Meister's Apprenticeship*

THE HARPER

He who ne'er ate bread with tears,
Or through a night of misery
Has sat upon his bed and wept,
He knows you not, you heavenly powers.

You lead us wretches into life.
Let poor men stumble into guilt,
And then you leave us to our pain,
For all pay for their guilt on earth.

MIGNON

Kennst du das Land, wo die Zitronen blühn,
Im dunkeln Laub die Gold-Orangen glühn,
Ein sanfter Wind vom blauen Himmel weht,
Die Myrte still und hoch der Lorbeer steht,
Kennst du es wohl? Dahin! Dahin
Möcht ich mit dir, o mein Geliebter, ziehn.

Kennst du das Haus? Auf Säulen ruht sein Dach,
Es glänzt der Saal, es schimmert das Gemach,
Und Marmorbilder stehn und sehn mich an:
Was hat man dir, du armes Kind, getan?
Kennst du es wohl? Dahin! Dahin
Möcht ich mit dir, o mein Beschützer, ziehn.

Kennst du den Berg und seinen Wolkensteg?
Das Maultier sucht im Nebel seinen Weg,
In Höhlen wohnt der Drachen alter Brut,
Es stürzt der Fels und über ihn die Flut;
Kennst du ihn wohl? Dahin! Dahin
Geht unser Weg! O Vater, lass uns ziehn!

MIGNON

You know the land where lemon flowers bloom,
And oranges gleam gold in leafy gloom?
A gentle breeze wafts from an azure sky,
The myrtle stands still, and the laurel grows high:
My dearest love, is this a place you know?
For there, oh there, with you I wish to go.

You know the house? A pillar holds each beam;
The great hall glitters, and the chambers gleam;
And marble statues stare, and look at me:
Alas, poor child, what have they done to thee?
 Oh, my guardian, is this a place you know?
For there, oh there, with you I wish to go.

You know the mountains' path and misty shroud?
The mule must seek its way through veils of cloud;
In caverns dwell the dragons' ancient race;
Torrents plunge down the precipice's face:
There lies our way—is it a place you know?
For there, oh there, my father, let us go!

SELIGE SEHNSUCHT

Sagt es niemand, nur den Weisen,
Weil die Menge gleich verhönet:
Das Lebend'ge will ich preisen
Das nach Flammentod sich sehnet.

In der Liebesnächte Kühlung,
Die dich zeugte, wo du zeugtest,
Überfällt dich fremde Fühlung
Wenn die stille Kerze leuchtet.

Nicht mehr bleibest du umfangen
In der Finsternis Beschattung,
Und dich reisset neu Verlangen
Auf zu höherer Begattung.

Keine Ferne macht dich schwierig,
Kommst geflogen und gebannt,
Und zuletzt, des Lichts begierig,
Bist du Schmetterling verbrannt.

Und so lang du das nicht hast,
Dieses: Stirb und werde!
Bist du nur ein trüber Gast
Auf der dunklen Erde.

BLESSED YEARNING

Tell it to no one but the wise,
For low minds are quick to mock:
I praise the living soul that yearns
To find its death in flames.

In the balmy nights of love
When you were begotten, and beget,
Strange emotions spring within you
As the quiet candle shines.

No longer do you languish, bound
By the shadows of the night,
And afresh your longing sweeps you
To a higher consummation.

Now no distance daunts your striving,
Spellbound, you begin to soar,
And at last, mad for the flame,
You are burned up like a moth.

And as long as you do not know
That *to die* is *to become*,
You are just a wretched visitor
On this dark earth.

4

FRIEDRICH SCHILLER
(1759-1805)

Schiller is considered second only to Goethe among German writers, and noted especially as a playwright and philosophical poet. His first play, *The Robbers* (1781), exemplifies the attitudes of the Storm and Stress movement. With Goethe, who was his close friend, he shared an interest in folk material and the Middle Ages (reflected in "The Glove").

DER HANDSCHUH

Vor seinem Löwengarten,
Das Kampfspiel zu erwarten,
Sass König Franz,
Und um ihn die Grossen der Krone,
Und rings auf hohem Balkone
Die Damen in schönem Kranz.

Und wie er winkt mit dem Finger,
Auftut sich der weite Zwinger,
Und hinein mit bedächtigem Schritt
Ein Löwe tritt
Und sieht sich stumm
Rings um,
Mit langem Gähnen,
Und schüttelt die Mähnen
Und streckt die Glieder
Und legt sich nieder.

Und der König winkt wieder,
Da öffnet sich behend
Ein zweites Tor,
Daraus rennt
Mit wildem Sprunge
ein Tiger hervor.
Wie der den Löwen erschaut,
Brüllt er laut,
Schlägt mit dem Schweif
Einen furchtbaren Reif
Und recket die Zunge,
Und im Kreise scheu
Umgeht er den Leu

The Glove

At his lion pit one day,
Waiting for the fray,
Sat King Franz.
The greatest lords of the land were there,
And above, the circle of ladies fair
Made a garland of elegance.

And his finger signals to begin:
The cage doors open wide,
And with a measured stride
A lion steps in,
And looks without a sound
All around;
He yawns with disdain
And shakes his mane
And stretching his limbs, lies down
On the ground.

And the king signals once more:
A second door
Is quickly sprung,
And a tiger plunges,
Wildly lunges.
When the lion meets his eyes
He roars out,
Begins to loll his tongue,
And in an arc to flail
His terrible tail;
He snarls and stalks about;
Round and round he prowls,
Then warily lies
On the other side and growls.

Grimmig schnurrend,
Drauf streckt er sich murrend
Zur Seite nieder.

Und der König winkt wieder,
Da speit das doppelt geöffnete Haus
Zwei Leoparden auf einmal aus,
Die stürzen mit mutiger Kampfbegier
Auf das Tigertier;
Das packt sie mit seinen grimmigen Tatzen,
Und der Leu mit Gebrüll
Richtet sich auf—da wird's still,
Und herum im Kreis,
Von Mordsucht heiss,
Lagern die greulichen Katzen.

Da fällt von des Altans Rand
Ein Handschuh von schöner Hand
Zwischen den Tiger und den Leun
Mitten hinein.

Und zu Ritter Delorges spottender Weis'
Wendet sich Fräulein Kunigund:
"Herr Ritter, ist Eure Lieb so heiss,
Wie Ihr mir's schwört zu jeder Stund,
Ei, so hebt mir den Handschuh auf!"

Und der Ritter in schnellem Lauf
Steigt hinab in den furchtbarn Zwinger
Mit festem Schritte
Und aus der Ungeheuer Mitte
Nimmt er den Handschuh mit keckem Finger.

And the king signals anew:
Then double cages spew
Two leopards in the ring,
And they viciously spring
On the tiger, lusting gore;
He slashes with his claws,
And the lion gets up with a roar;
There is a dreadful pause
As the great cats circle round;
They crouch on the ground,
And bare their teeth,
And, burning to kill, form a grisly wreath.

Then from the gallery above
A fair hand drops a glove—
Between tiger and lion lets it fall,
In the midst of them all.

And to Sir Delorges, in a mocking way,
Lady Kunigunde turns to say,
"Sir Knight, if your love for me is so great
As you've sworn to me, both early and late,
Why then, retrieve that glove for me."

And the knight as quick as can be
Enters the fearful place
With a firm pace,
And from the monsters' very claws
With deft fingers the glove withdraws.

Und mit Erstaunen und mit Grauen
Sehen's die Ritter und Edelfrauen,
Und gelassen bringt er den Handschuh zurück.
Da schallt ihm sein Lob aus jedem Munde,
Aber mit zärtlichem Liebesblick—
Er verheisst ihm sein nahes Glück—
Empfängt ihn Fräulein Kunigunde.
Und er wirft ihr den Handschuh ins Gesicht:
"Den Dank, Dame, begehr' ich nicht!"
Und verlässt sie zur selben Stunde.

DER SPAZIERGANG

Sei mir gegrüsst, mein Berg mit dem rötlich strahlenden Gipfel!
    Sei mir, Sonne, gegrüsst, die ihn so lieblich bescheint!
Dich auch grüss ich, belebte Flur, euch, säuselnde Linden,
    Und den fröhlichen Chor, der auf den Ästen sich wiegt,
Ruhige Bläue, dich auch, die unermesslich sich ausgiesst
    Um das braune Gebirg, über den grünenden Wald—
Auch um mich, der, endlich entflohn des Zimmers Gefängnis
    Und dem engen Gespräch, freudig sich rettet zu dir.
Deiner Lüfte balsamischer Strom durchrinnt mich erquickend,
    Und den durstigen Blick labt das energische Licht.
Kräftig auf blühender Au erglänzen die wechselnden Farben,
    Aber der reizende Streit löset in Anmut sich auf.
Frei empfängt mich die Wiese mit weithin verbreitetem Teppich,
    Durch ihr freundliches Grün schlingt sich der ländliche Pfad,
Um mich summt die geschäftige Bien, mit zweifelndem Flügel

And every lady and knight
Watches with horror and fright
As he calmly retrieves the glove.
From every mouth his praises rise
But from Lady Kunigunde's eyes
Come tender looks of love—
Clearly he's won his case.
And he throws the glove in her face:
"For your thanks, lady, I do not care!"
And he leaves her then and there.

THE WALK (1797)

Greetings to you, my mountain, with your ruddy, glowing summit!
    And greetings, sun, you lovely giver of light!
And to you, dear meadow, hello! Hello to you, whispering lindens,
    And to all the merry singers perched in your boughs—
And you, calm blue, who pour yourself down the sky forever
    Around the bare mountain, over the greening woods—
Around me as well! escaped at last from my study prison
    And the bondage of words, I find joyful refuge in you.
The resinous edge of your breeze cuts through me, reviving my senses,
    The vigorous light refreshes my thirsty eyes.
Thrilling across the mead, the hues of wildflowers shimmer,
    The clash of colors resolves in harmonious delight.
The fields fling out their carpets to the far horizon in welcome;
    A country path meanders through the friendly green;
Around me the bees buzz at their trade, while with aimless flutter

Wiegt der Schmetterung sich über dem rötlichen Klee,
Glühend trifft mich der Sonne Pfeil, still liegen die Weste,
   Nur der Lerche Gesang wirbelt in heiterer Luft.
Doch jetzt brausts aus dem nahen Gebüsch, tief neigen der Erlen
   Kronen sich, und im Wind wogt das versilberte Gras.
Mich umfängt ambrosische Nacht: in duftende Kühlung
   Nimmt ein prächtiges Dach schattender Buchen mich ein,
In des Waldes Geheimnis entflieht mir auf einmal die Landschaft,
   Und ein schlängelnder Pfad leitet mich steigend empor.
Nur verstohlen durchdringt der Zweige laubigtes Gitter
   Sparsames Licht, und es blickt lachend das Blaue herein.
Aber plötzlich zerreisst der Flor. Der geöffnete Wald gibt
   Überraschend des Tags blendendem Glanz mich zurück.
Unübersehbar ergiesst sich vor meinen Blicken die Ferne,
   Und ein blaues Gebirg endigt im Dufte die Welt.
Tief an des Berges Fuss, der gählings unter mir abstürzt,
   Wallet des grünlichten Stroms fliessender Spiegel vorbei.
Endlos unter mir seh ich den Äther, über mir endlos,
   Blicke mit Schwindeln hinauf, blicke mit Schaudern hinab;
Aber zwischen der ewigen Höh und der ewigen Tiefe
   Trägt ein geländerter Steig sicher den Wandrer dahin.
Lachend fliehen an mir die reichen Ufer vorüber,
   Und den fröhlichen Fleiss rühmet das prangende Tal.
Jene Linien, sieh! die des Landmanns Eigentum scheiden,
   In den Teppich der Flur hat sie Demeter gewirkt.
Freundliche Schrift des Gesetzes, des menschenerhaltenden Gottes,
   Seit aus der ehernen Welt fliehend die Liebe verschwand!
Aber in freieren Schlangen durchkreuzt die geregelten Felder,
   Jetzt verschlungen vom Wald, jetzt an den Bergen hinauf
Klimmend, ein schimmernder Streif, die länderverknüpfende Strasse,
   Auf dem ebenen Strom gleiten die Flösse dahin.
Vielfach ertönt der Herden Geläut im belebten Gefilde,
   Und den Widerhall weckt einsam des Hirten Gesang,
Muntre Dörfer bekränzen den Srom, in Gebüschen verschwinden

A butterfly wanders above the clover blooms.
I feel the sun's hot shafts, the western sky lies peaceful,
    Only the lark's song trembles in the bright air.
Now whispers arise from the neighboring bushes, deeply the alders
    Bow their heads, the grass sways silver in the wind.
Ambrosial glooms embrace me: and in the fragrant coolness
    Shadowy beeches extend a magnificent roof.
Now in the shades of the forest I suddenly lose the landscape
    And begin to ascend, led by a serpentine path.
Through the trellis of leafy branches, only a furtive glimmer
    Of light can break, and laughing blue peep in.
All at once the veil is parted, an opening in the forest
    Startles me with the blinding light of day.
The mighty vista surges out before my eyes,
    And purple mountains rim the world in mist.
Far down at the base of the precipice plunging abruptly beneath me
    The green stream's liquid mirror welters by.
Below me, a boundless sea of air, a boundless sea above me—
    Look up, grow dizzy; shudder looking down:
But in between those high and low extremities,
    A safe railed stair to take the traveller on!
Lush fringe of laughing farmland mounts to meet me,
    The valley boasts of its happy industry.
See how those lines, that mark the bounds of farmers' holdings
    Turn fields to carpets from Demeter's loom!
A caring God decreed possession's friendly limits
    Since love took wing and fled the brazen world.
But looping in freer curves across the fields' straight edges,
    Now biting into woods, now climbing up
To the hills, a gleaming stripe, the road that binds the country,
    The level river glides its rafts along.
Often the cheerful fields ring with the bells of cattle,
    And Echo wakens at the herdsman's song;
Lively hamlets deck the stream, while others vanish

Andre, vom Rücken des Bergs stürzen sie gäh dort herab.
Nachbarlich wohnet der Mensch noch mit dem Acker zusammen,
   Seine Felder umruhn friedlich sein ländliches Dach,
Traulich rankt sich die Reb empor an dem niedrigen Fenster,
   Einen umarmenden Zweig schlingt um die Hütte der Baum.
Glückliches Volk der Gefilde! Noch nicht zur Freiheit erwachet,
   Teilst du mit deiner Flur fröhlich das enge Gesetz.
Deine Wünsche beschränkt der Ernten ruhiger Kreislauf,
   Wie dein Tagewerk, gleich, windet dein Leben sich ab!
Aber wer raubt mir auf einmal den lieblichen Anblick? Ein fremder
   Geist verbreitet sich schnell über die fremdere Flur.
Spröde sondert sich ab, was kaum noch liebend sich mischte,
   Und das Gleiche nur ists, was an das Gleiche sich reiht.
Stände seh ich gebildet, der Pappeln stolze Geschlechter
   Ziehn in geordnetem Pomp vornehm und prächtig daher.
Regl wird alles, und alles wird Wahl, und alles Bedeutung,
   Dieses Dienergefolg meldet den Herrscher mir an.
Prangend verkündigen ihn von fern die beleuchteten Kuppeln,
   Aus dem felsigten Kern hebt sich die türmende Stadt.
In die Wildnis hinaus sind des Waldes Faunen verstossen,
   Aber die Andacht leiht höheres Leben dem Stein.
Näher gerückt ist der Mensch an den Menschen. Enger wird um ihn,
   Reger erwacht, es umwälzt rascher sich in ihm die Welt.
Sieh, da entbrennen in feurigem Kampf die eifernden Kräfte,
   Grosses wirket ihr Streit, Grösseres wirket ihr Bund.
Tausend Hände belebt ein Geist, hoch schläget in tausend
   Brüsten, von einem Gefühl glühend, ein einziges Herz,
Schlägt für das Vaterland und glüht für der Ahnen Gesetze,
   Hier auf dem teuren Grund ruht ihr verehrtes Gebein.
Niedcr steigen vom Himmel die seligen Götter und nehmen
   In dem geweihten Bezirk festliche Wohnungen ein.
Herrliche Gaben bescherend erscheinen sie: Ceres vor allen
   Bringet des Pfluges Geschenk, Hermcs den Anker herbei,
Bacchus die Traube, Minerva des Ölbaums grünende Reiser,

Among the leaves, or plunge down the mountain's back.
Here a man and his land can still live together as friendly neighbors,
    His fields resting peacefully round his farmhouse roof,
The familiar vine twining its tendrils over the low-hanging window,
    The cottage safe in the staunch embrace of a tree.
Lucky dwellers on the land! Not yet awake to freedom,
    Content to share your farmland's simple laws,
Plagued by no desires beyond the harvest's cycle,
    A day's work, or a life, for you are one.
But quick—where is that lovely view? What alien spirit
    Suddenly makes these fields more alien still?
Now things stand cold and distinct, that so recently lovingly mingled,
    And like insists on being matched with like.
I see adumbrations of ranks, the haughty family of poplars,
    Marshalled—magnificent, splendid in orderly pomp.
All is by rule, all is intentional, all has a meaning—
    Such vast subservience implies a lord:
Shining on the horizon, the gleaming spires proclaim him,
    The towered city springs from rocky seed.
The fauns of the ancient woods are driven into the desert,
    But devotion lends a higher life to stone.
Man is brought closer to man, and the world brought closer around him—
    More keenly awakened, set turning more lively within;
See, in fiery struggle his passionate powers kindle—
    Strife's works are great, but Concord's greater still.
One spirit animates a thousand hands, *one* feeling—
    One heart—beats high within a thousand breasts,
Beats for the fatherland, burns for the ancient laws of the forebears
    Whose honored bones lie deep in this dear earth.
The gods descend from heaven, and these blessed regions
    Become for them a consecrated home.
As they appear, they offer glorious gifts: first Ceres
    Donates the plow; Hermes, the anchor, next;
Bacchus the grape, Minerva the green branch of the olive,

Auch das kriegrische Ross führet Poseidon heran,
Mutter Cybele spannt an des Wagens Deichsel die Löwen,
    In das gastliche Tor zieht sie als Bürgerin ein.
Heilige Steine! Aus euch ergossen sich Pflanzer der Menschheit,
    Fernen Inseln des Meeres sandtet ihr Sitten und Kunst,
Weise sprachen das Recht an diesen geselligen Toren,
    Helden stürzten zum Kampf für die Penaten heraus.
Auf den Mauern erschienen, den Säugling im Arme, die Mütter,
    Blickten dem Heerzug nach, bis ihn die Ferne vetschlang.
Betend stürzten sie dann vor der Götter Altaren sich nieder,
    Flehten um Ruhm und Sieg, flehten um Rückkehr für euch.
Ehre ward euch und Sieg, doch der Ruhm nur kehrte zurücke,
    Eurer Taten Verdienst meldet der rührende Stein:
"Wanderer, kommst du nach Sparta, verkündige dorten, du habest
    Uns hier liegen gesehn, wie das Gesetz es befahl."
Ruhet sanft, ihr Geliebten! Von eurem Blute begossen,
    Grünet der Ölbaum, es keimt lustig die köstliche Saat.
Munter entbrennt, des Eigentums froh, das freie Gewerbe,
    Aus dem Schilfe des Stroms winket der bläulichte Gott.
Zischend fliegt in den Baum die Axt, es erseufzt die Dryade,
    Hoch von des Berges Haupt stürzt sich die donnernde Last.
Aus dem Felsbruch wiegt sich der Stein, vom Hebel beflügelt;
    In der Gebirge Schlucht taucht sich der Bergmann hinab.
Mulcibers Amboss tönt von dem Takt geschwungener Hämmer,
    Unter der nervigten Faust spritzen die Funken des Stahls.
Glänzend umwindet der goldne Lein die tanzende Spindel,
    Durch die Saiten des Garns sauset das webende Schiff.
Fern auf der Reede ruft der Pilot, es warten die Flotten,
    Die in der Fremdlinge Land tragen den heimischen Fleiss;
Andre ziehn frohlockend dort ein, mit den Gaben der Ferne,
    Hoch von dem ragenden Mast wehet der festliche Kranz.
Siehe, da wimmeln die Märkte, der Kran von fröhlichem Leben.
    Seltsamer Sprachen Gewirr braust in das wundernde Ohr.
Auf den Stapel schüttet die Ernten der Erde der Kaufmann,

And Poseidon brings his most spirited charger along;
Mother Cybele hitches her lions to the shafts of her coach to draw her,
    An honored citizen, through the welcoming gates.
Sacred pillars! From you the founders of mankind arose,
    You sent morality and art to the ends of the earth;
From these genial gates the law was wisely spoken,
    And heroes rushed in their Penates' defense.
On the walls of the city, the mothers appeared, holding their infants,
    Watching the troops march away, till they passed from sight,
Then flung themselves down in supplication before the altars
    Praying for victory, glory, and safe return.
Victory and glory you won, but your fame returned home without you;
    A touching stone sums up your earthly deeds:
"Traveler, when you come to Sparta, tell our story—
    We lie here as the laws of Fate decreed."
Rest peacefully, beloved men! From your blood's richness
    The olive flourishes, the good seed springs.
Now industry joyfully kindles, delighting in its possessions;
    From the river's sedge glitters the sky-blue god.
The ax hisses and bites the tree, the dryads murmur,
    Down from the heights crashes the thundering load.
The rock breaks from its craggy seams, lifted by engines,
    The miner plunges into the mountain's side.
Mulciber's anvil rings with the regular blows of the hammer,
    Under the brawny fist fly the sparks of steel.
Gleaming, the golden flax winds on the dancing spindle,
    Through chords of yarn the weaving shuttle hums.
Far out in the roadstead the pilot calls, the ships are waiting
    To bear the homeland's goods to foreign shores;
Others approach in triumph, laden with foreign riches,
    Flaunting festive garlands from their towering masts.
See, where the markets are swarming, those centers of life and gladness,
    A wonderful babel of language bursts on the ear.
The merchant pours out the produce of all the earth on his counters—

Was dem glühenden Strahl Afrikas Boden gebiert,
Was Arabien kocht, was die äusserste Thule bereitet,
    Hoch mit erfreuendem Gut füllt Amalthea das Horn.
Da gebieret das Glück dem Talente die göttlichen Kinder,
    Von der Freiheit gesäugt wachsen die Künste der Lust.
Mit nachahmendem Leben erfreuet der Bildner die Augen,
    Und vom Meissel beseelt redet der fühlende Stein.
Künstliche Himmel ruhn auf schlanken jonischen Säulen.
    Und den ganzen Olymp schliesset ein Pantheon ein.
Leicht wie der Iris Sprung durch die Luft, wie der Pfeil von der Sehne,
    Hüpfet der Brücke Joch über den brausenden Strom.
Aber im stillen Gemach entwirft bedeutende Zirkel
    Sinnend der Weise, beschleicht forschend den schaffenden Geist,
Prüft der Stoffe Gewalt, der Magnete Hassen und Lieben,
    Folgt durch die Lüfte dem Klang, folgt durch den Äther dem Strahl
Sucht das vertraute Gesetz in des Zufalls grausenden Wundern,
    Sucht den ruhenden Pol in der Erscheinungen Flucht.
Körper und Stimme leiht die Schrift dem stummen Gedanken
    Durch der Jahrhunderte Strom trägt ihn das redende Blatt.
Da zerrinnt vor dem wundernden Blick der Nebel des Wahnes,
    Unt die Gebilde der Nacht weichen dem tagenden Licht.
Seine Fesseln zerbricht der Mensch. Der Beglückte! Zerriss er
    Mit den Fessln der Furcht nur nicht den Zügel der Scham!
Freiheit ruft die Vernunft, Freiheit die wilde Begierde,
    Von der heilgen Natur ringen sie lüstern sich los.
Ach, da reissen im Sturm die Anker, die an dem Ufer
    Warnend ihn hielten, ihn fasst mächtig der flutende Strom,
Ins Unendliche reisst er ihn hin, die Küste verschwindet,
    Hoch auf der Fluten Gebirg wiegt sich entmastet der Kahn;
Hinter Wolken erlöschen des Wagens beharrliche Sterne.
    Bleibend ist nichts mehr, es irrt selbst in dem Busen der Gott.
Aus dem Gespräche verschwindet die Wahrheit, Glauben und Treue
    Aus dem Leben, es lügt selbst auf der Lippe der Schwur.
In der Herzen vertraulichsten Bund, in der Liebe Geheimnis

What the burning fields of Africa bring forth,
What Arabia prepares, what farthest Thule produces:
    Delightful wares brim Amalthea's horn.
There fortune joined with talent bears immortal children:
    Nurtured in freedom, all the arts of joy grow tall.
The sculptor delights the eye with reality's perfect image,
    And stone, given life by the chisel, feels and speaks.
An artificial heaven rests on slim Ionian columns,
    And all Olympus fills a Pantheon.
As light as a rainbow arching through heaven, or the flight of an arrow,
    The bridge's yoke leaps over the boisterous stream.
Yet in his study the thinker plots his subtle circle,
    Takes by surprise the powers of creation itself,
Tests the forces of matter, the hates and loves of the magnet,
    Traces light and sound through the ether and the air,
Seeks the familiar law in chance's awful confusion,
    Seeks the unmoving pole in appearance's flux.
Writing lends body and voice to thought that has long been silent—
    It crosses the centuries' stream on the speaking page;
Then before our wondering eyes, the cloud of delusion disperses
    And daylight quells the specters of the night.
Man breaks his fetters! Oh happy had he never broken,
    Along with the chain of fear, the curb of shame!
"Freedom!" cries our Reason: "Freedom!"—our baser passions
    Would fiercely burst from Nature's holy bond.
Then the storm tears loose the anchor that held man safe in harbor,
    And he is in the rip-tide's mighty grasp;
He's swept into eternity, loses sight of the coastline,
    His dismasted bark totters on mountainous waves;
Behind the clouds are hidden the steadfast stars of the Dipper,
    Now all is lost—even the God in his heart.
From speech, truth disappears; from life, all faith and honor,
    And sacred oaths pollute the lips with lies.
Into the heart's most faithful bonds, into love's secrets,

Drängt sich der Sykophant, reisst von dem Freunde den Freund,
    Auf die Unschuld schielt der Verrat mit verschlingendem Blicke,
        Mit vergiftendem Biss tötet des Lästerers Zahn.
Feil ist in der geschändeten Brust der Gedanke, die Liebe
        Wirft des freien Gefühls göttlichen Adel hinweg.
Deiner heiligen Zeichen, o Wahrheit, hat der Betrug sich
        Angemasst, der Natur köstlichste Stimmen entweiht,
Die das bedürftige Herz in der Freude Drang sich erfindet;
        Kaum gibt wahres Gefühl noch durch Verstummen sich kund.
Auf der Tribüne prahlet das Recht, in der Hütte die Eintracht,
        Des Gesetzes Gespenst steht an der Könige Thron.
Jahrelang mag, jahrhundertelang die Mumie dauern,
        Mag das trügende Bild lebender Fülle bestehn—
Bis die Natur erwacht und mit schweren ehernen Händen
        An das hohle Gebäu rühret die Not und die Zeit
Einer Tigerin gleich, die das eiserne Gitter durchbrochen
        Und des numidischen Waldes plötzlich und schrecklich gedenkt,
Aufsteht mit des Verbrechens Wut und des Elends die Menschheit
        Und in der Asche der Stadt sucht die verlorne Natur.
O, so öffnet euch, Mauern, und gebt den Gefangenen ledig!
        Zu der verlassenen Flur kehr er gerettet zurück!
Aber wo bin ich? Es birgt sich der Pfad. Abschüssige Gründe
        Hemmen mit gähnender Kluft hinter mir, vor mir den Schritt.
Hinter mir blieb der Gärten, der Hecken vertraute Begleitung,
        Hinter mir jegliche Spur menschlicher Hände zurück.
Nur die Stoffe seh ich getürmt, aus welchen das Leben
        Keimet, der rohe Basalt hofft auf die bildende Hand.
Brausend stürzt der Giessbach herab durch die Rinne des Felsens,
        Unter den Wurzeln des Baums bricht er entrüstet sich Bahn.
Wild ist es hier und schauerlich öd. Im einsamen Luftraum
        Hängt nur der Adler und knüpt an das Gewölke die Welt.
Hoch herauf bis zu mir trägt keines Windes Gefieder
        Den verlorenen Schall menschlicher Mühen und Lust.
Bin ich wirklich allein? In deinen Armen, an deinem

The sycophant thrusts, tearing friend from friend;
Betrayal leers at Innocence with hungry glances,
    The slanderer murders with his venomed fang.
Thought is up for sale in the dishonored bosom,
    Love's feelings, free and Godlike, are cast out.
Deceit, Oh Truth, has taken up your holy symbols,
    Defiling Nature's own most precious voice
That the needy heart discovers in a flush of gladness;
    True feeling has no voice, is scarcely known.
Justice swaggers in court, harmony in the cottage,
    The ghost of law stands at the throne of the king.
For years, for centuries, the mummy may remain,
    The lying facade appears with the fullness of life—
Till Nature awakes and with heavy brazen hand collapses
    The hollow pile—Necessity and Time:
As a tigress caged, bursting her iron bars, remembers
    Suddenly, fearfully, her old Numidian woods,
So mankind, mad with crime and pain, might stand again
    And seek lost Nature in the city's ruins.
Oh, open up, ye walls, and give the prisoner freedom!
    Let him go back in peace to his long-lost fields!
But—where am I? The path is lost; before me, behind me,
    Steep cliffs and gaping chasms block my way.
I've left behind the companionship of gardens and hedges,
    And every vestige of the hand of man.
I see only primitive matter heaped about, the matrix
    Of higher life, basalt for a shaping hand.
Roaring, the torrent plunges down through its rocky channel
    Forcing its angry way under roots of trees.
The place is desolate, chilling, wild; in the lonely heavens
    An eagle hangs, sole link of the earth with the clouds.
Not the forlornest note of human joy or sorrow
    Carries up to me on any breeze's wing.
Then am I now truly alone? Ah, no! In your arms once again,

Herzen wieder, Natur, ach! und es war nur ein Traum,
Der mich schaudernd ergriff mit des Lebens furchtbarem Bilde;
    Mit dem stürzenden Tal stürzte der finstre hinab.
Reiner nehm ich mein Leben von deinem reinen Altare,
    Nehme den fröhlichen Mut hoffender Jugend zurück!
Ewig wechselt der Wille den Zweck und die Regel, in ewig
    Wiederholter Gestalt wälzen die Taten sich um;
Aber jugendlich immer, in immer veränderter Schöne
    Ehrst du, fromme Natur, züchtig das alte Gesetz.
Immer dieselbe, bewahrst du in treuen Händen dem Manne,
    Was dir das gaukelnde Kind, was dir der Jüngling vertraut,
Nährst an gleicher Brust die vielfach wechselnden Alter:
    Unter demselben Blau, über dem nämlichen Grün
Wandeln die nahen und wandeln vereint die fernen Geschlechter,
    Und die Sonne Homers, siehe! sie lächelt auch uns.

In your heart, dearest Nature! The other was only a dream
That held me frozen in horror at life's terrifying image;
    Those shadows have vanished now with the plunging vale.
Pure again I renew my life at your pure altar,
    And renew the joyous heart of hopeful youth!
Forever the will is revising its goals and its rules, forever
    Our actions revolve on themselves in varying form;
But ever young, in ever-changing forms of beauty,
    You, blessed Nature, mind the ancient law;
Ever the same, you hold for man in your faithful keeping
    What the youth, what the tricksy child entrusted to you,
And at the same breast you nourish the varied, evolving ages:
    Under the same blue, over the same green,
The races near to us and far proceed together
    And Homer's sun—see! also smiles on us!

FROM *ON NAIVE AND SENTIMENTAL POETRY* (1795)

If we recall how beautiful the natural world of the Greeks was, how trustingly they lived in the freedom of nature under their blessed heaven; how very close their ideas, feelings, and manners lay to nature's own simplicity; and what a striking reflection of all this can be seen in their literature — then it is astonishing to find there so little of that *sentimental* interest that we moderns devote to scenes and characters of nature. The Greeks are, to be sure, to the highest degree accurate and detailed in their descriptions of these things, but not a bit more so, and with no more feeling, than they are in describing a piece of clothing, a shield, armor, furniture, or some other manufactured product. In their love for the object they seem to make no distinction between that which exists in itself and that which exists through human art and will. Nature seems to interest their understanding and their curiosity more than their moral feeling; they are not attracted to it with such fervor, such sensibility, such sweet melancholy as we moderns are. Indeed, their personification of nature's various phenomena as gods, representing natural effects as the acts of independent beings, negates precisely that serene necessity which makes nature so fascinating to us. Their impatient imagination passes over nature as they hurry on to the drama of human life. Nothing pleases them but character, action, fate, and manners; and whereas *we,* in certain states of mind, might wish to give up our privilege of free will — which exposes us to so much strife with ourselves, so much anxiety and error — in exchange for blind obedience to necessity, the Greek imagination, quite the reverse, is busy protecting human nature even into the inanimate world and giving the will an influence where blind necessity once ruled.

Where does this difference in spirit come from? How is it that we — who are so infinitely surpassed by the ancients in everything natural — precisely here pay a higher degree of homage to nature, are more deeply attached to it, and can embrace even the inanimate world with the warmest feeling? *This* is the reason: for us nature has disappeared from within man, and we encounter it again in its true form only on the outside, in the inanimate world. Far from any superior *harmony with nature,* it is on the contrary the *incompatibility with nature* of our circumstances, life, and manners, that leads us to seek in the physical world something we cannot hope to find in the moral world: the satisfaction of our awakening impulse for truth and simplicity, which, like the moral fabric from which it has arisen, remains incorruptible and indelible in every human heart. This explains why our love of nature is so closely related to our nostalgia for the bygone days of childhood and childlike innocence. Since childhood is the only unspoiled nature we meet in civilized life, it is not surprising that every trace of nature outside of us leads us back to our childhood.

It was quite otherwise for the ancient Greeks. Their culture had not advanced so far that nature was lost from it. Their whole society was based on sensibility rather than on an artificially constructed system; their mythology itself was the product of naive feeling — the offspring of a happy imagination, not the dismal faculty of reason, as is the religion of modern nations. Thus, since the Greek had not lost the nature within himself, he felt no surprise when he encountered it outside of himself, nor did he have any pressing need for some external object in which to find nature again. At one with himself and happy in the sense of his own humanity, he would necessarily cherish this humanity as his greatest attribute, and try to bring everything else closer to it; while *we,* at odds with ourselves and unhappy in our experience of humanity, desire nothing so urgently as to escape this humanity and remove from our eyes such a misshapen form.

The feeling pointed out here is thus not the same as that which the ancients experienced; it comes much closer to being that *which we have for the ancients.* We have a feeling *for* naturalness; their feeling *was* natural. Certainly a different feeling filled Homer's soul when he told of his saintly swineherd's hospitality to Ulysses, than stirred young Werther's soul when he read the same passage after a dull party. Our feeling for nature is like a sick person's attraction to health.

When nature gradually disappears from human life as *experience* and as *subject* (both active and passive), we see it emerge in literature as *idea* and *object.* The nation which has carried furthest both separation from nature and reflection upon that separation, must have been the one most

forcefully struck by the phenomenon of the naive, to the point even of
giving it a name. This nation was, I believe, the French. But the feeling for
the naive and the interest in it is naturally much older, going back to the
beginning of our moral and aesthetic corruption. The change in feeling is,
for example, already quite striking in Euripides, when he is compared with
his predecessors, especially Aeschylus; yet Euripides was the favorite poet
of his time. The same revolution may be seen in the ancient historians.
Horace, the poet of a cultivated and corrupt era, praises the peaceful bliss
of his Sabine farm, and he may be called the true founder of the sentimental
type of writing, just as he is the still unsurpassed exemplar of it. Similarly,
in Propertius, Virgil, and others, one finds traces of this same vein of feeling
— less in Ovid, who lacked the fullness of heart for it and who in his exile
at Tomi painfully missed the pleasures that Horace on his Sabine farm so
willingly dispensed with.

Traditionally, poets are *guardians* of nature. When they are no longer
quite able to fill this role, and already feel in themselves the destructive
influence of arbitrary and artful forms, or have had to struggle against them,
they present themselves as *witnesses* and *avengers* of nature. They will
either *be* nature, or, nature being lost, they will *seek* it. From this circumstance
emerge two quite distinct kinds of poetry, which between them encompass
and exhaust the entire sphere of poetry. All true poets will — depending on
the time in which they flourish, or on the chance circumstances that have
influenced their overall education and shifting mental state — be classified
as either *naive* or *sentimental.*

The poet of a naive, intellectually rich young world — as well as he who,
in a later, more sophisticated civilization, comes closest to him — is austere and
chaste, like the virginal Diana in her woods; shunning all intimacy, he flees the
heart that seeks him and the desire that would embrace him. The matter-of-fact
way in which he handles his subject often gives the impression of coldness. The
object occupies him completely; his heart is not to be found right on the surface
like a base metal, but rather in the depths, like gold. Like the Deity behind the
universe, he remains hidden behind his work; he *is* the work, and the work is
himself; indeed, a reader must be either unworthy of such a work, or inadequate
to it, or tired of it, if he asks about the author.

That is how Homer, for example, among the ancients, appears, and Shakespeare among the moderns:two natures totally different and separated by an unbridgeable gulf of years, yet absolutely identical in just this quality. When I first read Shakespeare as a very young man, I was angered by his coldness, his lack of feeling, which allowed him to joke in the midst of the highest pathos, to spoil the most heartrending scenes, as in *Hamlet, King Lear,* or *Macbeth,* by introducing a fool — a coldness which sometimes made him pause when my feelings were rushing on, and sometimes carried him onward unfeelingly when my heart longed to tarry. Misled as I was, through my acquaintance with modern poets, into the practice of immediately seeking the poet in the work, of meeting *his* heart, of reflecting familiarly *with him* on his object — in short, of seeing the object in the subject — I found it intolerable that here the poet would always slip through my fingers and never give me an account of himself. I studied Shakespeare and admired him wholeheartedly for many years before I learned how to reach his individuality. I was not yet capable of understanding nature first hand. I could only bear its image reflected through the reason and organized by rules, and, for that, the sentimental authors of France and Germany between about 1750 and 1780 were exactly the right subjects. Moreover, I am not ashamed of this childish judgment, because mature critics at that time made similar pronouncements, and were naive enough to publish them to the world.

The same thing happened to me with Homer, whom I came to know at a later period. I still remember the striking passage in the sixth book of the *Iliad,* when Glaucus and Diomedes meet in battle and, recognizing their relation as host and guest, exchange gifts. This touching picture of piety, in which the laws of *hospitality* were obeyed even in war, can be compared with a scene of *chivalrous generosity* in Ariosto, where two rival knights, Ferrau and Rinaldo, Saracen and Christian, after a mighty battle, covered with wounds, make peace and mount the same horse together to pursue the fugitive Angelica. Both examples, different though they may be in other respects, are almost identical in their effect on our hearts — both depict a splendid victory of civility over the passions, and touch us with the simplicity of their feelings. But what totally different methods the two poets use in describing these similar incidents. Ariosto, citizen of a later world far removed from such simplicity of manners, in relating this scene cannot hide how amazed and touched he is. He is overwhelmed by a sense of the distance between such behavior and the manners of his own age. All at once he leaves off the objective depiction of the scene and speaks out in his own voice. . . . "Oh, the nobility of those old chivalric manners!"

. . . But *of* all this there is no trace in Homer; he goes right along in his dry, matter-of-fact way as if he were describing an everyday occurrence —indeed, as if he himself had no heart in his breast:

> Zeus must have addled Glaucus' wits; without a thought
> He swapped his gòlden armor, worth a hundred oxen,
> For Diomedes', which was bronze, worth only nine.

A sophisticated age hardly affords a place for poets of this naive sort. In fact they are scarcely possible any longer, or at least possible only if they *careen wildly* across their age and by some lucky fate are protected from its maiming influence. They can never arise from society itself; but outside of it they still occasionally appear — rather like aliens, to be sure, objects of wonder, and like ill-bred children of nature, a source of vexation to ordinary folk. Salutary as these rare manifestations are for the artist who studies them and for the true connoisseur who properly appreciates them, they cause little joy in general for their age. Whereas we wish to be rocked and carried along by the muses, these bear the seal of sovereignty on their brow. The critics, regular policemen of good taste, hate them as destroyers of boundaries, who ought to be suppressed; for even Homer may have only the strength of his thousand-and-more-year reputation to thank, that these inquisitors of taste allow him credit; and as it is they find it hard enough to maintain their rules against his example, and his authority against their rules.

I have said that a poet either *is* nature, or he *seeks* nature. The former is the naive, the latter the sentimental poet.

The poetic spirit is immortal and ever-present in mankind; it can only disappear with humanity and human nature itself. For, while man strays from the simplicity, truth, and necessity of nature through the free play of his fancy and understanding, not only does the path back to nature always stand open to him, but a powerful and indelible impulse — the moral — impels him irresistibly back; and it is precisely with this impulse that the poetic faculty stands in the closest relationship. This faculty thus is not lost immediately, as soon as natural simplicity is lost, but simply works in another direction.

Nature is still the only flame that kindles the poetic spirit; from it alone that spirit derives its power, to it alone that spirit speaks, even in sophisticated authors who have a full grasp of culture. Any other mode of operation is foreign to poetry; hence, incidentally, it is quite incorrect to give the name of poetry to any of the so-called productions of wit, although, misled by the influence of French literature, we have for some time been guilty of that confusion. I repeat: the poetic spirit, even in the present sophisticated state of civilization, still receives its power from nature; it is only the relationship of the two that is different.

As long as humanity remains pure nature (and this does not mean crude nature), it functions as a simple, sentient unity, a harmonious whole. Sense and reason, receptive and active faculties, have not yet split into their separate functions — much less do they contradict one another. Man's feelings are not the formless play of chance, his thoughts are not the empty play of fantasy; the former arise from the law of *necessity,* the latter arise from *truth.* When man has entered the state of civilization, and art has laid its hand upon him, he loses the harmony of his *senses,* and can now display only a *moral* unity, that is, a striving toward unity. The agreement between his feeling and his thought, which in his primal state had a *real* existence, now has a strictly *ideal* existence; it is no longer within him, but outside of him — a thought that first has to be realized, no longer a fact of his life. If we now apply the concept of poetry (which is simply the *most complete expression possible of humanity*) to the two states just described, we see that in the state of natural simplicity, where man still functions with all his powers together, as a harmonious unity, and where consequently his whole nature is completely expressed as reality itself, the poet's role is *to represent reality* as fully as possible; whereas here in the state of civilization,where this harmonious cooperation of his whole nature is only an idea, the poet's role is to elevate reality to the ideal, or, what amounts to the same thing, to *represent the ideal.* And these are the only two possible ways, generally speaking, that the poetic genius can manifest itself. The difference between the two is obvious, but there is a higher concept that contains both, and it should not be too surprising if this concept should coincide with the idea of humanity.

Here is not the place to pursue this idea, which only a separate discussion can set in its full light, but whoever can make a comparison between the ancient and modern poets, according to their spirit and not just according to their accidental forms, will easily be convinced of its truth. The ancients move us through nature, through sensuous truth, through a living presence; the moderns move us through ideas.

The way followed by the modern poets is moreover the same as that which mankind in general, both as individuals and as a whole, must take. Nature makes man a unified being; art separates and divides him, but through the ideal he returns to wholeness. Now, since the ideal is infinite and never attainable, civilized man can never become perfect in *his* way, as the natural man can in his. He would thus always be infinitely inferior to the natural man's perfection, if all that we considered was the relation in which each stood to his own way and potential maximum. But if we compare the ways themselves with each other, it becomes clear that the goal toward which man *strives* through culture is infinitely superior to that which he *attains* through nature alone. Thus one derives his merit from complete attainment of a finite end, the other achieves his from approaching one of infinite magnitude. Since only the second of these ways involves *degrees* and *progress,* the relative merit of the civilized person in general can never be determined though such a person taken individually is necessarily at a disadvantage with respect to one in whom nature works in all its perfection. But inasmuch as the ultimate goal of mankind cannot be attained except by progress, and the natural man cannot make progress except by seeking culture and hence by following the way of civilization, there is really no question, when one remembers this ultimate goal, as to which is the superior of the two.

Everything that has been said here of the two different forms of humanity applies to the two kinds of poets that correspond to them.

We should thus not try to compare the ancient and modern — the naive and sentimental — poets at all, or at any rate we should compare them only in terms of a higher concept that includes both (and actually there is one such concept). Of course, if one begs the question by one-sidedly basing a definition of poetry on the ancients, nothing is easier — and nothing more meaningless — than to rank the moderns lower. If we define as poetry only what has uniformly affected simple nature at all times, then we automatically deny the name of poetry precisely to those noble and original beauties in which the moderns most highly excel, for these are precisely the places in which they speak to the child of civilization, and have nothing to say to the simple child of nature. Whoever is not already prepared to move beyond reality into the realm of the ideal will regard the most substantial riches of poetry as empty show, and the loftiest poetic flights as exaggeration. No reasonable person would rank any of the moderns as Homer's equal for the qualities which make him great, and it sounds rather ridiculous to hear a Milton or a Klopstock honored with the name of a "modern Homer." But just as little could one base a case for any of the ancients, least of all Homer, on the excellences that distinguish the modern poets. I would express it this way: the ancients excel in the art of the clearly defined; the moderns, in the art of the infinite.

WILHELM HEINRICH WACKENRODER
(1773-1798)

A boyhood friend of Ludwig Tieck, Wackenroder wrote the first manifesto of German Romanticism, *Effusions from the Heart of an Art-Loving Monk* (1796-7), which contains such characteristically Romantic attitudes as admiration for the Middle Ages, a virtually religious reverence for art, and a rejection of logical reason and analysis in favor of feeling. His portrait of the musician Berglinger is a thinly veiled picture of his own aesthetic aspirations.

FROM *EFFUSIONS FROM THE HEART OF AN ART-LOVING MONK*

Longing for Italy

By a curious chance, I have preserved among my things the following note, written when I was quite young and obsessed with the wish someday to see *Italy,* the beloved land of art:

Day and night my soul thinks only of the beautiful, bright regions that appear in all my dreams and beckon to me. Will my wish, my longing, always be in vain? So many people travel there and come back, and yet do not realize where they have been, and what they have seen; for no one loves so fervently as I that land and its native art.

Why does it lie farther from me than a few days' journey on foot? — so that I might kneel down before the undying works of the great artists, and confess to them all my admiration and love? — and so their spirits might hear it, and greet me as their faithful pupil.

If I happen to see maps belonging to my friend, I can never resist poring over them with excitement; mentally I wander through cities, towns, and villages — and, ah! feel only too soon that it is all just imagination.

I have no wish for brilliant success on this earth; but shouldn't I be given the chance just for a while to live entirely for you, oh holy art?

> Must I thus forever pine
> Brooding till my life is spent?
> Is it destiny's design
> To make this weight, these thoughts of mine
> An endless plague of discontent?
>
> Lost and lonely from the start,
> Am I to exile dedicated?
> Happy he who, born for art,
> Never doubts that life and heart
> Are to its service consecrated.

Far from my reach my fortune lies,
Seeming never to grow near —
Yea, and many doubts arise,
Yet still the stars wheel through the skies —
At last! At last! my dream is here!

No more delaying,
After long dreaming,
After deep calm,
Through wood and heath,
Through meadows in bloom,
To my true home!

Flying to meet me
With blessings to greet me,
Genius comes
In his dazzling wreath,
Leading the weary
To delicious peace,
To joy and calm,
To art's own home!

Some Words About Universality, Tolerance, and Love of Mankind in Art

The Creator who made our earth and everything in it held the whole terrestrial ball in his single glance, and poured out his blessing in a stream over the whole round world. But from His mysterious workshop he scattered over the globe the infinitely varied seeds of thousands of different things, that bear infinitely varied fruits; and to his glory the greatest, most brightly varied of gardens springs up. Miraculously he launches his sun in its precise orbit about the earth, so that its rays, hitting the globe at a thousand different angles, bring forth from the marrow of the earth the most various creations under every sector of heaven. With equal eye, in *one* great moment, He considers the work of His hands, and receives with pleasure the offerings of all animate and inanimate nature. The roaring of the lion is as acceptable to Him as the call of the reindeer, and the aloe smells as sweet to Him as the rose and the hyacinth.

Likewise human beings came from His creating hand in thousands of different forms: — not even the brothers of *one* household know one another or understand one another; they speak different languages, and are baffling to each other: — but He knows them all, and is pleased with them all; with equal eye he considers the work of His hands and receives the offerings of all nature.

He hears the voices of men conversing among themselves of heavenly things in many various ways, and knows that all, — all, even though contrary to what they know and will, — still are trying to express *Him,* the inexpressible.

So too He hears the various voices of men's inner feelings in various parts of the world and various eras, and hears how they quarrel and fail to understand one another; but for the Eternal Spirit everything dissolves in harmony. He knows that a person uses whatever speech he has been endowed with — that each person expresses his inner self however he can and must: if in their blindness they quarrel with each other, still He knows and understands that each is right by his own lights; He looks with pleasure on each and all, and rejoices in the brilliant motley.

Art is the name for the flower of human feeling. In ever-changing form it springs up from the various parts of the earth toward Heaven, and from all these blossomings there wafts up to the Father of All, Who holds in His hand the round earth and everything therein, *one* perfectly blended perfume.

He recognizes in every work of art, from every part of the world, a spark of the Heavenly fire that, emanating from Him, has passed through the human breast and into man's little creations, from which it feebly reflects back to the Great Creator. To Him the Gothic cathedral is as pleasing as the Greek temple, and the barbarous war music of the savage sounds as lovely as exquisite choirs and hymns.

And if I then turn from Him, the infinite, in the boundless reaches of the Heavens, back to earth, and look around me at my fellow men — ah! it is enough to make me cry out in despair, so little do they strive to become like their great eternal exemplar in Heaven. They quarrel with each other, and misunderstand each other, and fail to see that they are all hurrying toward the same goal, because each has his feet planted firmly in his own little spot, and can't lift his eyes to survey the whole.

People are so near-sighted, they can't understand that our earth has its opposite poles, and that every person is a different pole. They always assume that the spot they are standing on is the unique hub of the universe, and their minds lack the wings to circle the universe and to catch in *one single* look of their eyes the self-existent entity of the world.

And in the same way they consider *their* feeling the touchstone of everything beautiful in art, and make their absolute pronouncements about everything like a judge from his bench, without realizing that nobody has appointed them to judge, and that anyone who has been condemned by them has an equal right to set up his own opinions in opposition.

Why not condemn the Indian for speaking his own language instead of ours?

And by the same reasoning, will you condemn the Middle Ages because they did not build the same kind of churches as ancient Greece?

Oh, try to project yourself into souls different from your own, and you will see that you and your erring brothers have obtained your talents from the same hand! Realize, then, that each being can shape forth its own creations only with the strengths that it has received from Heaven, and that each person's works must accord with his own nature. And if you cannot project your *feelings* into every unfamiliar being, and actually *experience* their works in your mind, at least you can try to reach out to these different persuasions indirectly through the logical conclusions of the understanding.

If the sowing Hand of Heaven had cast the germ of your soul in the African desert, then you would have pronounced shining black skin, a broad flat face, and short curly hair to be essential components of the highest beauty for the whole world, and you would have regarded the first white people you saw as laughable or repulsive. Had your soul fallen a few hundred miles further east, on the soil of India, then you would have sensed the mysterious spirit which, inaccessible to our perceptions, hovers in the little strangely shaped, many-armed gods of that region; and, if you saw the Venus de Medici, you would not know what to make of it. And had it pleased Him in Whose power you stood and stand to cast you among the South Sea Islanders, you would have found a deep meaning in every wild drumbeat, and in the rude, piercing beat of the music, not a syllable of which you can now comprehend. But in any of these cases, would you have received the gift of creativity or the gift of artistic genius from a source other than the eternal and universal one to which you are even now indebted for everything you hold dear?

The multiplication table of reason follows the same laws in all nations of the earth, the only difference being that it is applied to ever-widening fields in one place, to very narrow ones in others. In the same way, *artistic feeling* is simply one and the same heavenly ray of light, which, however, is broken into a thousand different colors in the many-faceted prism of sensuous perception in different parts of the world.

Beauty: a wonderfully strange word! Just try finding new words for every single artistic feeling, for every single work of art! A different coloration plays over each, and for each, different nerves were created in the human frame.

But from this one word, through the arts of the understanding, you spin out a harsh *system,* and would force all people to feel according to your rules and prescriptions — and you yourself do not feel!

Whoever *believes a system,* has driven universal love out of his heart! Still, the intolerance that comes from feeling is more bearable than intolerance from the understanding: better to be the dupe of *superstition* than of a *system.*

Can you force the melancholy person to find pleasure in comic songs and merry dance? Or the person of cheerful disposition to willingly offer up his heart to tragic horrors?

Then leave every mortal being and every people under the sun to their own belief and their own bliss! And rejoice if others rejoice — even if it is over something, though dearest and most precious to them, that you don't understand enough to appreciate.

We, the children of this century, have the advantage of standing on the peak of a high mountain, able to look out over many lands and many ages, which stretch in every direction at our feet. So let us then profit by this good fortune, and, as our clear eyes stray over all times and peoples, let us strive always to sympathize with *the human* in all their multifarious feelings and works of feeling.

Every being strives towards what is most beautiful: but, unable to escape out of himself, each sees the highest beauty only in himself. Just as every mortal eye perceives the rainbow in a different way, so every person receives from the world around him a different image of beauty. But the universal, original beauty, that in moments of transcendent vision we can only *name,* not reveal through words, is known to Him who made the rainbow and the eye that sees it.

I began my discourse with Him, and to Him I return again: in the same way, the spirit of art, the spirit of everything, flows from Him, and through the earth's atmosphere, and redounds to Him again as an offering.

How and in What Way the Works of the Great Artists of this World Should Be Understood and Used for the Good of the Soul

Often I hear the childish and frivolous world complain that God has sent such a small number of really great artists into the world; impatiently the ordinary mind peers into the future to see if our Heavenly Father will not let another glorious generation of brilliant artists arise. But I say, it is not true that the earth has borne too few great artists; indeed, a lifetime is not enough for a mere mortal to look at and comprehend the work of a single one of their number; and truly there are far, far too few who are capable of fervently understanding and (what is the same thing) of intensely honoring the work of those beings formed of finer clay.

Museums are treated like fairs where new wares are judged, praised or mocked in passing; yet they should be as temples, where in uplifting solitude and silent humility we should honor great artists as the highest among mortals, and in deep contemplation of their work refresh our souls in the bright sunshine of the rapturous thought and feeling they inspire.

I liken the enjoyment of great art to prayer. Heaven does not love him who prays only to discharge a routine duty, who mouths words without thought and boastfully measures his devotion by the beads of his rosary. But he is beloved of Heaven who with humble longing waits for those chosen hours when the mild beams of Heaven descend upon him freely, rending the ordinary and insignificant mortal shell that covers our earthly mind, and freeing and revealing his more noble inner self; then he kneels and in silent ecstasy he turns his open heart toward the glory of heaven and drinks his fill of ethereal light, and when he arises — more joyful, and more sweetly sad than before, his heart fuller and lighter — he turns his hand to some great good work. — That is the real meaning I find in prayer.

And I believe a person should approach great art in just the same way, if he is to find in it, as he should, the well-being of his soul. I call it blasphemous when in some worldly hour a man staggers from the echoing laughter of his friends to spend some few minutes in a nearby church, out of mere habit, to speak to God. And it is a similar sacrilege in such an hour to cross the threshold of a house in which are kept for all eternity, bearing silent witness to the dignity of mankind, the most wonderful creations of which human hands are capable. Wait, as you do with prayer, for that sacred hour when the grace of Heaven illuminates your inner self with revelation; only then will your soul merge with the work of artists. Their magic forms will forever be silent and opaque if you look at them indifferently; your heart must first speak strongly to them if you would have them speak to you and exert their full power over you.

Works of art are by their nature as little suited as the thought of God to the course of daily life; they surpass the ordinary and the routine, and we rise to them with full hearts so that in our eyes, all too often befogged by the atmosphere of this world, we create them as they are in their lightest essence.

Anyone can learn to read the letters of the alphabet; anyone can let chronicles tell him the history of times gone by, and can retell them; and anyone can study a philosophical system and comprehend laws and truths;

—for letters exist only so that the eye may recognize their form; and formulas and events are of interest to us only as long as our mind's eye is working to grasp them and know them; as soon as we make them our own, mental activity ceases, and we simply indulge only when it pleases us, in a lazy unfruitful review of our treasures. But it is not so with the work of mighty artists. They do not exist for the eye to see; but so that we go into them with a welcoming heart and live and breathe in them. A magnificent painting is not a paragraph in a textbook, which I throw aside like a useless shell when with little effort I have taken out the meaning of the words; with great works of art enjoyment continues without end. We feel we can keep penetrating deeper and deeper into them. They continue to stimulate our imagination and we cannot foresee a time when our spirit may exhaust them. In them burns an eternally living flame which dims before our eyes.

Impatiently I hurry past the first impression, because the surprise of novelty — which many, always snatching at new sensations, deem to be the main attraction of art — has always been for me a necessary evil of the first encounter. True enjoyment requires a calm and quiet frame of mind and it takes the form not of exclamations and applause but only of a deep inner response. It is a holy festive day for me when, gravely and with soul prepared, I go to view noble works of art; often I return to them again and again. They are imprinted on my mind, they will always be with me in my imagination like a blessed charm for the comfort and the awakening of my soul for all eternity.

He whose finer nerves have become receptive to the mysterious attraction which lies hidden in art will often be deeply moved where another passed by indifferently; and he will have the good fortune to find many occasions for such wholesome excitement and stimulation. I know that often, preoccupied with other thoughts, I have walked through some beautiful arcade of lofty columns whose gracious majesty compelled my eyes to turn involuntarily to them, and, bowing inwardly, I would then continue on my way, my heart suffused with joyous peace, my soul richer than it had been before.

But above all, it is wrong to put oneself arrogantly and presumptuously above the exalted artists and condescendingly judge them: a foolish endeavor of man's vain pride: *Art* is *above* man: we can only honor and admire the glorious work of those dedicated to it, and open our whole hearts to them to cleanse and liberate all our feelings.

6

LUDWIG TIECK
(1773-1853)

One of the key members of the Schlegel circle of "Early Romantics," Tieck is especially noted for the psychological subtlety and complex use of irony in his dramas and fiction. The early short story *Blond Eckbert* (1797) is one of the first "artificial folk tales," a popular genre among Romantic writers. The farcical *Puss in Boots* (1797) is a light-hearted example of Romantic irony and an illustration of the Romantic rejection of bourgeois values.

Blond Eckbert

In a region of the Harz mountains lived a knight, whom people usually called simply "Blond Eckbert." He was about forty years old, barely of medium height, with short, light blond hair that lay straight and thick around his pale, sunken face. He lived quietly to himself and never got involved in his neighbors' quarrels; in fact, he was seldom seen outside the walls of his little castle. His wife loved solitude as much as he did, and the two of them seemed very much in love with one another: their only regret, as they often said, was that Heaven had not blessed their marriage with children.

Eckbert entertained guests only occasionally, and when he did, the normal course of life was hardly altered on their account: moderation dwelt there, and frugality herself seemed the housekeeper. At those times Eckbert was cheerful and animated; only when he was alone he seemed to withdraw within himself and fall into a certain quiet, reserved melancholy.

No one came so often to the castle as Philipp Walther, a man to whom Eckbert was attached because they seemed to think in just the same way, and who had become his best friend. Walther's home was actually in Franconia, but he often stayed more than half the year in the neighborhood of Eckbert's castle, collecting plants and rocks, which he studied and classified. He lived on a small private income and was dependent on no one. Eckbert often accompanied him on his solitary walks, and with every passing year a deeper friendship grew between them.

There are moments when it is painful for a person to keep from a friend some secret which up to that time he has done his best to hide. At such times the soul feels an irresistible impulse to open itself up completely, to unlock its innermost depths to the friend, and so to make him even more a friend. At such moments even the most sensitive soul will reveal itself to another; and sometimes it may also happen that another will shrink from the knowledge.

Autumn had arrived. One foggy evening Eckbert sat with his wife Bertha and his friend Walther before a blazing fireplace. The flames cast a bright glow around the room and flickered up on the ceiling; the night looked black through the windows, and the trees outside shivered in the damp cold. Walther was not looking forward to his long walk home that evening, and Eckbert suggested that he spend the night. They could pass a long evening in good talk, and then Walther could sleep in one of the guest rooms. Walther accepted; now wine and supper were brought in, wood was added to the fire, and the friends' conversation grew more lively and more intimate.

When the supper things were cleared and the servants had gone away, Eckbert took Walther's hand and said, "My good friend, I would like my wife to tell you the story of her childhood; I think you'll find it quite unusual."

"Gladly," Walther said; and they all sat down again around the fire.

It was now exactly midnight; the moon shone fitfully through the ragged clouds. "I hope you won't take what I'm about to tell you amiss," began Bertha. "My husband says that you are so high-minded, it wouldn't be right to conceal anything from you. Please believe me, what I'm about to tell you is no fairy tale, however strange it may sound.

"I was born in a small village; my father was a poor herdsman. My parents were not good managers, and they often did not know where the next day's bread was coming from. But what disturbed me much more was that my father and my mother often quarreled about their poverty and blamed one another bitterly. And besides this, they were constantly telling me that I was a stupid, foolish child, who couldn't do the simplest job properly. And in fact I was extremely awkward and clumsy—I dropped everything, I couldn't sew or spin or help with the housework. The only thing I understood very well was my parents' poverty. Often I would sit in a corner and fill my mind with daydreams of how I would help them if I suddenly became rich, how I would shower them with gold and silver, and revel in their surprise; then again I would imagine ghosts floating up, that would show me buried treasures or give me little pebbles that would turn into precious stones. In short, I lost myself in the most wonderful fantasies, and when I had to get up again to help with something or to carry something, I was even more clumsy because my head was swimming with all those daydreams.

"Because I was such a useless burden in the household, my father was always cross with me, and he often treated me pretty badly. I seldom had a kind word from him. Well, when I was about eight years old, my parents decided that I really should do or learn something. My father believed that it was only stubbornness or laziness that made me waste my days so idly, so he made unspeakable threats to me, and when these had no effect, he beat me in the most horrible fashion, saying that this punishment would be repeated every day, as long as I remained such a useless creature.

"I cried bitterly the whole night through; I felt myself so utterly friendless, I felt so sorry for myself, that I wanted to die. I feared the break of day, I had absolutely no idea what I ought to do; I wished I were clever at all sorts of things and could not understand why I should be more simpleminded than the other children I knew. I was close to despair.

"As day began to break, I stood up and, scarcely realizing what I was doing, opened the door of our little cottage. I found myself in the open field, and soon was in some woods, before the day had fully dawned. I ran on headlong, without looking to either side; I never felt tired, because I kept thinking my father would catch me again and, angered by my running away, would treat me even more harshly.

"When I came out of the woods again, the sun was already pretty high; I saw something dark lying before me, covered by a thick mist. Sometimes I had to scramble over hills, sometimes go along a path that wound between rocks, and I now realized that I must be in the nearby mountains; and at that point, realizing my solitude, I began to feel frightened. For down on the plain I had never seen any mountains, and the mere word 'mountains,' when I heard it spoken, had a frightening sound to my childish ear. I didn't have the courage to turn back; my fear drove me onward; many times I looked around, terrified, when the wind gusted through the trees over my head, or when the distant sound of chopping echoed through the morning stillness. When at last I met some miners and mountaineers and heard their strange accents, I was ready to faint with terror.

"I passed through several villages and begged, because by now I was hungry and thirsty. When people asked me questions, I helped myself by answering pretty well. And so I walked on, it must have been four days, when I found myself on a little footpath that led me farther and farther away from the main road. The rocks around me now took on another, far stranger appearance. There were high cliffs, so close together that it looked as if a hard wind would blow them against each other. I didn't know if I should go on. On previous nights I had slept in the woods—for it was the warmest season—or in isolated shepherds' huts; but here I came upon no human dwelling and had no reason to expect any in this wild region. The cliffs became more and more frightful; I often had to go along close to the edge of dizzying precipices, and finally even the pathway under my feet was lost. I was now completely desolate; I cried and screamed, and my voice echoed through the rocky gorges in a frightful way. Now night fell, and I looked for a mossy spot to rest in. I couldn't sleep; through the night I heard the strangest noises, that I took sometimes for a wild animal, sometimes for the wind moaning through the rocks, and sometimes for strange birds. I prayed, and I did not fall asleep until it was almost morning.

"I awoke with the daylight in my face. A steep rock was in front of me, and I climbed up on it in the hope of discovering from there a way out of this wild place, and perhaps of seeing houses or people. But when I stood at the top, everything, as far as my eyes could see, was, just like my immediate surroundings, overcast with a gloomy vapor; the day was gray and dismal, and my eye could not discover a tree, a meadow, not even any shrubs, except for a few sad, solitary bushes that had sprung up in the narrow crevices of the rocks. It is impossible to describe the longing I felt just to catch sight of a human face, even if it were one I would be terrified of. At the same time I was racked with hunger, and I sat down and prepared to die. But after a little while the urge to live won out, and I hauled myself up and trudged onward, amid tears and broken-off sighs, for the whole day. Toward the end I was hardly conscious; weak and exhausted, I hardly wished to live and yet was afraid to die.

"Toward evening the landscape seemed to become a little more friendly. My thoughts and wishes revived, the urge to live awoke in all my veins. Now I thought I heard the faint sound of a mill in the distance; I increased my pace; and how glad, how buoyant I felt, as at last I really reached the end of the barren rocks. I once more saw woods and fields stretching out before me, with pleasant mountains in the distance. I felt as if I had stepped out of Hell into a paradise; my solitude and helplessness no longer seemed frightening.

"Instead of the mill I had hoped for, I stood at the edge of a waterfall, which I must admit diminished my joy a good bit. With my hand I scooped up a drink from the brook, when suddenly I heard something like a faint cough coming from a short distance away. Never have I been so pleasantly surprised as the moment when, going closer, I saw an old woman at the edge of the woods, apparently resting. She was dressed almost entirely in black, and a black hood covered her head and a good part of her face; in her hand was a crooked walking-stick.

"I came closer and asked her to help me. She told me to sit down beside her, and gave me some bread and a little wine. While I ate, she sang a hymn in a cracked voice. When she had finished, she told me I could follow her.

"I was very glad of this offer, however strangely the old woman's voice and looks struck me. She walked along pretty nimbly with her crooked stick, and she twisted up her face in such a droll fashion with each step that at first I couldn't keep from laughing. The wild rocks fell farther and farther behind us; we went across a pleasant field and then through a rather long stretch of woods. Just as we came out of the trees again, the sun was setting, and never in my life will I forget the sights and feelings of that evening. Everything was fused in the softest red and gold; the trees lifted their tops into the evening light, and the enchanting glow spread out over the fields. Every leaf was still; the clear sky looked like the open gates of paradise, and the murmur of little streams and occasional whispering of the trees gave a note of pensive joy to the calm, peaceful air. For the first time my young soul felt some intimation of the world and what it could offer. I forgot myself and my guide; my soul and my eyes were lost in a dream among the golden clouds.

"We now climbed a hill planted with birches, from the top of which we looked down into a green valley of birches; and in the middle of the trees stood a little cottage. A brisk barking came from the direction of the cottage, and soon a lively little dog ran up to the old woman wagging his tail. Then he came to me, looked me over from all angles, and turned back with friendly mien to the old woman.

"As we descended the hill, I heard a strange song that seemed to come from the cottage, and sounded like a bird. These were the words:

> Oh woodland solitude,
> How happy is your mood,
> Tomorrow as today
> You'll never pass away,
> I love your happy mood,
> Oh woodland solitude.

These few words were repeated over and over again. If I had to describe the way they sounded, it was as if a horn and an oboe were playing together in the distance.

"My curiosity was intensely aroused; without waiting for the old woman's invitation, I walked into the cottage with her. Twilight had already begun to fall; everything within was neatly arranged: some glasses stood in a cupboard, strange-looking vessels on a table, and in a shiny cage at the window hung a bird, which indeed had been singing the words. The old woman began to cough and gasp uncontrollably; she alternately patted the little dog and spoke to the bird, which answered her only with its usual song; and she acted quite as if I weren't there. As I was watching her I shuddered several times, for her features were in constant movement, and she was shaking her head as if from age, so that the whole time I could not tell how she really looked.

"When she had recovered herself, she lit a candle, set a tiny table, and brought out things for supper. Now she looked at me and told me to fetch up a wicker chair. So I sat exactly opposite her at the table, and the candle stood between us. She folded her gnarled hands and prayed aloud, during which she twisted her face up so that I almost burst out laughing again; but I carefully controlled myself, so she would not be angry.

"After supper she prayed again, and then showed me to a bed in a poor, cramped little room; she slept in the main room. I didn't stay awake long; I was half stunned with fatigue. But in the night I waked up several times, and then I heard the old woman coughing and talking to the dog, and occasionally the bird, who seemed to be dreaming, and sang only single words from its song. That, along with the birches that rustled at the window, and the song of a far-away nightingale, made such a strange mixture that it seemed to me not that I waked up, but only that I fell into another, even stranger dream.

"In the morning the old woman woke me and soon set me to work. I had to spin, and now I soon learned how; I also had to take care of the dog and the bird. I quickly learned to do housework, and became familiar with all its details. Soon everything seemed quite normal to me; it no longer crossed my mind that there was anything strange about the old woman, that her house was peculiar and situated far from other people, and that the bird was rather unusual. I was always struck with its beauty, though; its feathers gleamed with all possible colors, the most beautiful bright blue and the most fiery red shimmered on its neck and body, and when it sang, it puffed itself up proudly, so that it displayed its feathers even more splendidly.

"Often the old woman went away and didn't come back until evening. I would go out to meet her with the dog, and she would call me 'child' and 'daughter.' After a while I came to love her dearly: our minds become accustomed to everything, especially in childhood. In the evenings she taught me to read, a skill which I picked up easily, and which later became a source of endless pleasure to me in my solitude, for she had some old hand-written books that contained wonderful stories.

"Even now it's always strange for me to think of my life at that time: visited by no human creature, my whole world just that tiny family circle—for the dog and the bird made the same impression on me as dear old friends. I have never afterwards been able to remember the strange name of that dog as often as I used to call him.

"I had lived for four years this way with the old woman, and I was, I guess, about twelve years old, when she finally came to trust me more and revealed a secret to me. It was that the bird laid an egg every day which contained a pearl or some precious stone. I had already always noticed that she busied herself about the cage when I wasn't watching, but I had never thought much about it. Now she showed me how to collect these eggs when she was away, and to hide them carefully in the strange-looking vessels. After this she began to stay away longer—weeks, months—leaving me alone with enough food to last until her return. My little spinning wheel hummed, the dog barked, the wonderful bird sang, and all the while everything was so still all around, that the whole time I scarcely remember any rough winds or thunderstorms. No other person ever wandered by, no wild animal approached our house; I was contented and kept busy at my work day after day. I guess most people would be pretty fortunate if they could pass their entire lives so peacefully.

"From the little that I read, I painted for myself quite a marvellous picture of the world and the people in it, all based on myself and my tiny circle of acquaintance. When the tale was of lively, jolly folk, I couldn't help imagining that they were like the little dog; fine ladies always looked like the bird, and all old ladies like my own wonderful old woman. I had also read a little bit about love, and I now acted out in my fancy marvellous stories about myself. I imagined to myself the most handsome knight in the world and decked him out with every excellence, without actually knowing, after all of my pains, how he would look. But I could feel terribly sorry for myself if he didn't return my love; when that happened, I would compose long, tender speeches in my mind—sometimes even out loud—just to win his favor.—You smile! Of course we are all now past this time of youth.

"I now actually preferred being left alone, because then I was mistress of the house. The dog loved me and did everything I told him to; the bird answered all my questions with its song; my little spinning wheel turned merrily as ever; and so I never really had any desire to change. When the old woman came back from her long journeys, she praised the way I had performed my duties, saying that since I had been looking after the house it was much more neatly kept; she would exclaim happily about how much I had grown and how healthy I looked; and in short she behaved to me exactly as if I were her daughter.

"'You are a fine girl, my child!' she said to me once in a creaky voice; 'If you continue in the same way, things will always go well for you, but remember, it never fails that when a person wanders from the straight and narrow path, sooner or later punishment will catch up with him.' When she said this, I didn't pay much attention to it—I was not one to sit still long, either physically or mentally; but as I lay in bed at night it came to me again, and I could not understand what she had meant. I went over all the words carefully: I had read about riches, and at last it occurred to me that her pearls and precious stones might be valuable. This idea soon became clearer to me. But what could she mean by the 'straight and narrow path'? I just couldn't quite pin down the meaning of her words.

"I was now fourteen. It is unfortunate that just at the time when people attain reason, they lose the innocence of their souls. In short, it occurred to me that there was nothing to prevent my taking the bird and the jewels while the old woman was away, and seeking the world that I had read about. Then it might be possible for me to meet that supremely handsome knight who was always in my thoughts.

"At first this idea was nothing more than my other daydreams, but as I sat musing at my spinning wheel it kept coming back against my will, and I would lose myself in it until I could see myself all splendidly bejeweled and surrounded by knights and princes. After I had become lost in such thoughts, I usually became depressed when I looked about me again and found myself in the little cottage. But the old woman didn't trouble herself about me as long as I did my housework.

"One day as my hostess left the house she told me that this time she would stay away longer than usual, but that I should keep the household in good order and not let the time hang heavy on my hands. I felt a certain dread as she took her leave—somehow I felt I would never see her again. I watched her a long time as she went away, and did not know myself why I should be so anxious. It was almost as if I already knew what I was going to do, without clearly realizing it myself.

"Never had I taken care of the dog and the bird so diligently. I felt closer to them than ever. The old woman had already been gone several days when I got up one morning with the firm intention of leaving the cottage and setting out with the bird to seek what people call the world. My mind was racked and distressed: I wanted to stay there still, and then I hated the idea. There was a strange battle in my soul, like a struggle between two contrary spirits within me. At one moment I felt how beautiful this peaceful solitude was, then I would again become enraptured with thoughts of a new world with all its wonderful variety.

"I didn't know what to do with myself; the dog played about me in a carefree way, the sunshine spread cheerfully over the fields, the green birches sparkled. I had the feeling that I had to do something very quickly. So I grabbed the little dog, tied him fast in the cottage, and took the cage with the bird under my arm. The dog struggled and whined at this unaccustomed treatment; he looked at me with plaintive eyes; but I was afraid to take him with me. Then I took one of the vessels filled with jewels and hid it on me, but left the others.

"The bird turned its head in a strange way as I carried it to the door. The dog strained to come after me, but he had to stay behind.

"I avoided the way toward the wild rocks, and went in the opposite direction. The dog barked and whined continuously, which deeply disturbed me. The bird tried to start singing several times, but he seemed to have trouble with it while being carried.

"As I got farther away, the barking became fainter and fainter, and finally stopped altogether. I wept and almost turned back, but the urge to see new things drove me onward.

"I had already crossed some mountains and passed through some woods when evening came and I had to stop in a village. I went into the inn very timidly, but they gave me a room and bed, and I slept peacefully, except that I dreamt that the old woman was scolding me.

"My journey was fairly uneventful, though the farther I went the more painful became my thoughts of the old woman and the little dog. I couldn't help thinking that without my help he would probably starve to death. And, passing through woods, I often believed that I would suddenly meet the old woman. So with tears and sighs I put miles behind me. Whenever I rested and set the cage on the ground, the bird sang its wonderful song, and it vividly recalled to me the beautiful way of life I had left. Human nature is so forgetful, that I believed I had been less miserable on my earlier childhood journey than now; I would have gladly exchanged situations.

"I had sold some of the jewels and, after walking for many days, approached a village. As soon as I entered it I felt very strangely; I felt afraid without knowing why. But soon I realized that it was the very village where I was born. How astonished I was! How the tears of joy ran down my cheeks, from a thousand strange memories! Much had changed: new houses had been built, and others, that had been newly built at that time, had fallen in; I saw where a building had burned. Everything was much smaller, narrower, than I had expected. I was beside myself with joy at the prospect of seeing my parents again after so many years. I found their little house, the familiar doorway; the handle of the door was still exactly as it had been before. I felt as if I had pushed it only yesterday. My heart beat violently—I quickly opened the door; but all I saw was completely unfamiliar faces sitting around the room staring at me. I asked about the shepherd Martin, and was told that he and his wife had died three years ago. I left quickly and walked away from the village loudly weeping.

"I had had such lovely dreams of surprising them with my riches; through a strange chance, what I always only dreamed as a child had now actually come to pass—and now it was all in vain: they could not share my happiness, and what I had always hoped for most in life, was lost to me forever.

"I rented a little house with a garden in a pleasant city and hired a serving-maid. The world did not turn out to be so wonderful as I had imagined it, but my memories of the old woman and my earlier life were fading increasingly, and thus I managed to live quite contentedly.

"The bird had stopped singing now for a long time. I was therefore not a little startled when one night it suddenly began again, though with an altered song. It sang:

> Oh woodland solitude,
> How far away your mood!
> You've passed away
> Like yesterday—
> You were my only good
> Oh woodland solitude.

"I could not sleep all that night. All that had happened came back to me with new force, and more than ever before I felt that I had done wrong. When I got up, the sight of the bird was hateful to me. It kept looking at me, and its presence bothered me. And now it never left off its song, which it sang louder and shriller than before. The more I thought about the bird, the more I became filled with dread. Finally I opened the cage, stuck my hand in, grasped its neck, and squeezed my fingers together convulsively; it looked at me imploringly, but when I relaxed my hold, it was dead. I buried it in the garden.

"And now I gradually began to fear my serving-maid. Thinking back on my own history, I began to believe that at some time or other she might rob me or even murder me. Already for some time I had known a young knight, whom I liked more than anyone I had met, and so I gave him my hand. And with that, Herr Walther, my tale is ended."

"You should have seen her then," Eckbert hastily added—"her youth, her beauty, and the incredible charm her solitary upbringing gave her! She appeared before me like a vision, and I loved her beyond all measure. I had no fortune, but through her love I came into this present wealth. We moved here, and to this day have never regretted our union for a moment."

"But with all our chatter," Bertha continued, "look how late it's gotten! Let's go to bed!"

She stood up to go to her room. Walther kissed her hand and wished her a good night, saying, "Dear lady, thank you. I can picture you so clearly in my mind with that strange bird, and how you used to feed little *Strohmian*."

Walther went to bed too, and only Eckbert still paced restlessly to and fro in the room. "What fools we are!" he finally exclaimed to himself. "I myself first suggested that my wife tell her story, and now I already regret sharing our secret. Won't Walther abuse this confidence? Won't he tell someone else? Won't he, all too humanly, begin to covet our hoard of jewels and lay plans to steal them, while disguising his true feelings?"

It seemed to him that Walther had not been as cordial when he said good night, as one might have expected after such a confidence. Once the mind has felt the first tug of suspicion, it sees a confirmation in every trivial circumstance. Then Eckbert reproached himself for his ignoble mistrust of his best friend, and yet could not draw back from it. All night long he wrestled with these notions, and hardly slept.

Bertha was sick and did not appear at breakfast; Walter did not seem very concerned about it, and he seemed rather indifferent when he took leave of the knight. Eckbert could not understand this behavior. He went in to see his wife, who lay burning with fever. Telling the story the night before, she said, must have brought this on.

After that evening Walther seldom came to the castle of his friend, and even when he did come, he soon went away again after a little empty conversation. Eckbert was hurt to the quick by this behavior; he tried not to let Bertha and Walther notice anything, of course, but it was easy for anyone to see his inner turmoil.

Bertha's illness grew steadily worse. The doctor became anxious; the color disappeared from her cheeks, and her eyes burned more and more feverishly. One morning she called her husband to her bedside, and sent the maids away.

"Dear husband," she began, "I must tell you something that, insignificant trifle though it seems in itself, has ruined my health and driven me almost out of my mind. You know that, as often as I have talked about my childhood, I have never, in spite of all my efforts, been able to remember the name of the little dog I lived with for so many years. On that evening, when we were saying good night, Walter suddenly said to me, 'I can picture so clearly in my mind how you used to feed little *Strohmian.*' Was that chance? Did he guess the name, or did he know it and say it on purpose? And what connection does this man have with my fate? At times I struggled in my own mind, wondering whether I was only imagining this strange business. But it is true, all too true. It fills me with dread for a strange person to help me remember something like that. What do you say, Eckbert?"

Eckbert looked at his suffering wife with deep tenderness, but said nothing. He sat for a while in thought, then said a few comforting words to her and went out. In a little-used room he paced back and forth, indescribably agitated. For many years Walther had been his only companion, and yet now he was the one person in the world whose existence weighed on him and pained him. It seemed to him as if he would be happy and light-hearted if only this being could be removed from his path. He took his crossbow to distract himself and set out to hunt.

It was a raw, stormy winter day; deep snow lay on the mountains and bent down the branches of the trees. He scoured about till sweat stood on his forehead, but he found no game, and that deepened his ill humor. Suddenly he saw something move in the distance: it was Walther, gathering moss from trees. Scarcely realizing what he was doing, he took aim; Walter saw him and made a silent, threatening gesture, but at that instant the bolt flew and Walther pitched down headlong.

Eckbert felt lighthearted and calm, though a shudder made him turn back to his castle. He had a long way to go, because he had wandered far into the woods. When he reached home, Bertha was already dead; she had talked a great deal about Walther and the old woman before her death.

Eckbert now lived a long time in the greatest solitude. He had always been melancholy, for the strange story of his wife bothered him and he feared that some unlucky fate could happen. But now he went all to pieces. The murder of his friend stood continually before his eyes, and he lived under a continual gnawing guilt.

In order to distract himself, he occasionally went to the closest large town to seek company and entertainment. He wished to fill the void in his soul with some friend, yet when he thought again about Walther, he shrank from the idea of finding one, for he was convinced that he could not avoid being ill-fated in any other friendship. He had lived so long with Bertha in lovely serenity, and he had enjoyed the good fortune of Walther's friendship over so many years, and now both had been so suddenly snatched away, that many was the time his life seemed to him more like a strange fairy tale than a real human life.

A young knight, Hugo, became a close companion of the quiet, melancholy Eckbert and seemed to feel a real affection for him. Eckbert found himself wonderfully surprised to have fallen into a friendship with this knight much more quickly than he had expected. The two were now often together, the strange knight showed Eckbert every possible attention, one scarcely rode out without the other, they were always together at parties: in short, they seemed inseparable.

Eckbert was always happy only for brief spaces, for he felt keenly that Hugo liked him only through an error. Hugo didn't know him, was ignorant of his story; and he again felt the same urge to tell him everything in order to find out whether or not Hugo was really his friend. But then he was held back by doubt and the fear that he would be regarded with abhorrence. Many a time he was so convinced of his own unworthiness, that he believed no one could think well of him who knew him at all. Nevertheless, he could not resist the impulse: while they were out on a lonely ride he revealed to his friend his whole story and asked him then if he could love a murderer. Hugo was moved and tried to comfort him; Eckbert returned with him to the city light of heart.

But it seemed his special curse to conceive suspicion the moment he confided in anyone, for scarcely had they stepped into the hall together than he began not to like his friend's expression as it appeared under the many lights. He thought he could detect a malicious smile, and it struck him that Hugo talked with him very little, and paid attention to everyone else present but practically none to him. An older knight was at the gathering who had always seemed hostile to Eckbert and who had often inquired about his wife and his fortune in a peculiar way; Hugo made a point of joining him, and the two spoke secretively for a long time, often gesturing toward Eckbert. Eckbert now saw his suspicions confirmed; he believed himself betrayed, and was overcome with a terrible rage. As he stared fixedly at them, he suddenly saw Walther's face, all his gestures, the very image so well known to him; he continued to look at them and became convinced that it was none other than *Walther himself* who was speaking to the old knight. His horror was beyond description; he rushed away and out of the city in the middle of the night and, after much wandering, made his way back to his castle.

Now like a restless spirit he hastened from room to room; he could fix his attention on no object, but fell from one frightful image to another more frightful, and sleep would not close his eyes. Often he thought that he was mad and everything was a figment of his imagination; but then he remembered the way Walther looked, and everything became more of a riddle to him than ever. He decided to travel in the hope of settling his thoughts; by now he had given up forever the idea of friendship, the hope of social intercourse.

He set forth without any clear itinerary—in fact he thought very little about the countryside that lay before him. For several days he urged his horse along at a hard trot, until suddenly he saw that he had wandered into a labyrinth of rocky cliffs from which he could not find his way out. Finally he met a peasant who showed him a path that went by a waterfall. As a token of thanks he offered some coins to the peasant, who refused them. "What can this mean?" Eckbert said to himself—"It seems to me again that this is none other than Walther." With that he took another close look and it was none other than Walther. Eckbert spurred his horse as fast as it could gallop, through field and forest, until it collapsed in exhaustion beneath him. Undaunted by this, he continued his journey on foot.

Dazed, he climbed a hill; there was a sound nearby like the lively barking of a dog, and, above the whispering of the birches, he heard the wonderful tones of a song:

> Oh woodland solitude,
> Once more I feel your mood:
> Envy and pain
> Are gone again
> I feel your happy mood
> Oh woodland solitude.

This was too much for Eckbert's mind and senses. He couldn't find his way out of the maze: was he dreaming now, or had he merely dreamed that he had a wife named Bertha? The most marvellous things were mixed up with the most ordinary; all about him the world was bewitched, he had lost all control of thought and memory.

A crook-backed old woman with a walking stick was making her way slowly up the hill, coughing. "Have you brought my bird? My pearls? My dog?" she shrieked at him. "You see, evil punishes itself: your friend Walther, your Hugo—they were none other than me!"

"Dear God in heaven!" Eckbert said under his breath. "In what frightful solitude, then, I've passed my whole life!"

"And Bertha was your sister."

Eckbert fell to the ground.

"Why did she leave me so treacherously? Otherwise everything would have ended well and lovely. Her probation time was almost over. She was the daughter of a knight, who left her to be brought up by a herdsman— your father's daughter."

"Why have I always had a foreboding of these frightful things?" Eckbert cried.

"Because in your early childhood you once heard your father tell about them; on his wife's account he couldn't bring up this daughter in his own household, because her mother was another woman."

Eckbert lay on the ground delirious and dying. Stunned and confused, he heard the old woman talking, the dog barking, and the bird repeating its song.

Puss in Boots

A Fairytale in Three Acts, with Interludes, a Prologue and Epilogue

Characters

The King

The Princess, his daughter

Prince Nathaniel of Malsinki

Leander, court scholar

Hanswurst, court fool

A Valet

The Cook

Lorenz
Barthel } brothers and peasants
Gottlieb

Hinze, a cat

An Innkeeper

Kunz } peasants
Michel

Law, a bogeyman

A Soother

The Author

A Soldier

Two Hussars

Two Lovers

Servants

Musicians

A Peasant

The Prompter

A Shoemaker

A Historian

Fischer
Müller
Botticher } spectators
Leutner
Wiesener

Wiesener's Neighbor

Elephants

Lions

Bears

A Magistrate

Eagle and other Birds

A Rabbit

Partridges

Jupiter

Terkaleon

The Machinist

Ghosts

Monkeys

The Audience

PROLOGUE

(The scene is in the pit, the lamps are already lighted, the musicians are gathered in the orchestra. — The theater is filled, people are chattering with one another, more arriving, etc. Fischer, Müller, Schlosser, Boetticher in the pit.)

FISCHER. But I'm really curious. — Müller, what do you think of today's play?

MÜLLER. I would have sooner expected the sky to fall than to see such a play at *our* theater!

FISCHER. Do you know the play?

MÜLLER. Not in the least. — It has a strange title: *Puss in Boots.* — I certainly hope they aren't going to present a children's farce in the theater.

SCHLOSSER. Maybe it's an opera?

FISCHER. Anything but; on the playbill it says: a Children's Fairytale.

SCHLOSSER. A Children's Fairytale? But for Heaven's sake, are we children, that they present such plays to us? There isn't really going to be an actual cat coming onto the stage?

FISCHER. No doubt it's an imitation of the New Arcadians, a kind of Terkaleon —[1]

MÜLLER. That wouldn't be bad. I've been wanting for a long time to see a wonderful opera like that without music.

FISCHER. Why, without music, my friend, that sort of thing becomes ridiculous! We've gone beyond such childishness and superstition; after all, the Enlightenment has borne its proper fruits!

MÜLLER. Well then it's probably a domestic comedy, and it's only a joke, some sort of episode about a cat, a come-on, so to speak.

SCHLOSSER. To tell you the truth, I think the whole thing is a trick to spread certain sentiments — you know, put ideas into people's heads. See if I'm not right. A revolutionary play, from what I can tell.

FISCHER. I think so too — otherwise the thing would be in horribly bad taste. I must admit, I have never been able to believe in witches or ghosts, much less in Puss in Boots.

MÜLLER. The age for these phantoms is past. Here's Leutner; maybe he can tell us more.

(Leutner pushes his way through.)

LEUTNER. Good evening, good evening! How are you?

MÜLLER. Just tell us, what is today's play about?

(The music begins.)

LEUTNER. Is it already so late? Then I've come just in time. — About the play? I've just spoken with the author; he's in the theater and is helping the cat get dressed.

MANY VOICES. Is helping? — the author? — the cat? — Then a cat really is appearing?

LEUTNER. Yes, indeed; his name's even on the bill.

FISCHER. Who's playing him?

LEUTNER. Why, the foreign actor, the great man.

MÜLLER. Really? But how can anyone perform such stuff?

LEUTNER. The author thinks it will be a change, —

FISCHER. A fine change! Why not Bluebeard too, and Little Red Riding Hood? Ha! Outstanding subjects for drama!

MÜLLER. But how are they going to dress the cat? — And will he wear real boots?

LEUTNER. I'm just as curious as all of you.

FISCHER. But are we really going to let them put on such stuff for us? To be sure, we came out of curiosity, but we still have taste.

MÜLLER. I feel like stamping my feet.

LEUTNER. It's a little cold too. I'll start.

(He stamps his feet; the others accompany him.)

WIESENER *(on the other side)*. What's all this stamping for?

LEUTNER. To rescue good taste.

WIESENER. Well, I don't want to be left out.

(He stamps.)

VOICES. Quiet! We can't hear the music.

(Everyone stamps.)

SCHLOSSER. But we really ought to let them run through the play first, since we've already paid our money; afterwards we'll stamp so that they can hear us in the street!

ALL. No, now, now! — taste, — the rules, — art, — otherwise everything will break down!

LAMPLIGHTER. Gentlemen, will we have to call in the police?

LEUTNER. We've paid, we are The Public, and so we demand our own good taste and no monkey business!

AUTHOR *(behind the stage)*. The play will begin immediately.

MÜLLER. No play, — we don't want any play, — we want good taste, —

ALL. Taste! Taste!

AUTHOR. I'm puzzled; — what do you mean, if I may ask?

SCHLOSSER. Taste! — Are you an author and don't even know what taste is?

AUTHOR. Please consider, a young beginner. —

SCHLOSSER. We don't want to hear about beginners, — we want to see a proper play, — a tasteful play!

AUTHOR. Of what type? What kind?

MÜLLER. Domestic stories, abductions, brothers and sisters from the country, that sort of thing!

(The Author comes from behind the curtain.)

AUTHOR. Gentlemen, . . .

ALL. Is that the author?

FISCHER. He doesn't look much like an author.

SCHLOSSER. Smart-aleck.

MÜLLER. His hair is all wrong!

AUTHOR. Gentlemen, — pardon my boldness . . .

FISCHER. How can you write such plays? Why haven't you learned your profession?

AUTHOR. Lend me your ears for just one minute before you condemn me. I know that an honorable public must pass judgment on the author, that from you there is no appeal; but I also know the love for justice of an honorable public, that they won't frighten me away from a course in which I so badly need their charitable guidance.

FISCHER. He doesn't speak badly.

MÜLLER. He is more polite than I thought.

SCHLOSSER. He does have respect for the public.

AUTHOR. I am embarrassed to present the inspiration of my Muse before such enlightened judges, and only the artistry of our actors comforts me to some extent; otherwise I would immediately sink into despair.

FISCHER. I feel sorry for him.

MÜLLER. A good fellow!

AUTHOR. When I heard your honorable stamping, — nothing has ever frightened me so; I am still pale and trembling and cannot conceive how I could have been so bold as to appear thus before you.

LEUTNER. Then let's applaud!

(All applaud.)

AUTHOR. I just wanted to try — by humor if possible, by good-natured fun, even by plain buffoonery — to provide some amusement, since our newest plays so seldom give us an opportunity to laugh.

MÜLLER. That's true too!

LEUTNER. He's right, — that man.

SCHLOSSER. Bravo! Bravo!

ALL. Bravo! Bravo!

(All applaud.)

AUTHOR. Now you, honorable gentlemen, may decide whether my attempt is entirely to be rejected. Trembling, I withdraw, and the play will begin.

(He bows very respectfully and goes behind the curtain.)

ALL. Bravo! Bravo!

VOICE FROM THE BALCONY. *Da Capo!*

(Everyone laughs. The music begins again while the curtain goes up.)

ACT I

[Scene 1]

(Small room in a peasant hut. Lorenz, Barthel, Gottlieb. The cat Hinze lies on a stool by the stove.)

LORENZ. I think that, since our father is now departed, our small fortune can easily be divided. As you know, the blessed man left only three pieces of property: a horse, an ox and the cat over there. I, as the eldest, will take the horse; Barthel, the next after me, gets the ox; and then naturally the cat is left for our youngest brother.

LEUTNER *(in the pit)*. For Heaven's sake! Have you ever seen such an exposition! You can see just how low dramatic art has sunk!

MÜLLER. But I've understood everything really well.

LEUTNER. That's just the trouble; you have to insinuate it craftily — you can't just throw it into the spectator's face.

MÜLLER. But at least now we know where we stand.

LEUTNER. You don't have to know everything so quickly, though; it's precisely the getting into it little by little that's the best fun.

BARTHEL. I think, brother Gottlieb, you will also be satisfied with the division; you are unfortunately the youngest, and so you have to grant us some privileges.

GOTTLIEB. To be sure.

SCHLOSSER. But why isn't the juvenile court involved in the inheritance? What improbabilities!

LORENZ. So now we're ready to go, dear Gottlieb; farewell, don't let time hang heavy on your hands.

GOTTLIEB. Adieu.

(The brothers exit.)

GOTTLIEB *(alone)*. There they go — and I am alone. — Each of us has his cottage; Lorenz can till the fields with his horse; Barthel can slaughter and salt down his ox and live on it for a while; — but what am I, poor unfortunate, to do with my cat? — At most I can have a muff for the winter made from his fur; but I think he is still shedding. — There he lies, sleeping so peacefully. — Poor Hinze! We will soon have to part. I regret it; I raised him; I know him as well as I know myself. — But he will have to believe me; I can't help myself; I really will have to sell him. — He's looking at me as if he understood me; a bit more and I'll start to cry.

(He walks back and forth, lost in thought.)

MÜLLER. Well, now, don't you see that it's going to be a touching domestic drama? The peasant is poor and without money. In his extreme need he's going to sell his faithful pet to some sensitive young lady, and in the end that will be the foundation of his fortune. She falls in love with him and marries him. It's an imitation of *The Parrot* by Kotzebue; the bird has been made into a cat, and the rest of the play follows of itself.

FISCHER. Now that it's coming along this way, I'm also satisfied.

HINZE *(gets up, stretches, arches his back, yawns and then speaks)*. My dear Gottlieb, you have my profound sympathy.

GOTTLIEB *(astonished)*. What's that, cat, you're speaking?

THE CRITICS *(in the pit)*. The cat's speaking? — What is this?

FISCHER. It's impossible for me to get a realistic illusion here.

MÜLLER. I would rather never see another play the rest of my life, than be taken in like this again!

HINZE. Why shouldn't I be able to speak, Gottlieb?

GOTTLIEB. I would never have suspected it; in my entire life I've never heard a cat speak.

HINZE. Just because we don't butt into every conversation, you think we're nothing but dogs.

GOTTLIEB. I think you're here just to catch mice.

HINZE. If, in our dealings with man, we hadn't developed a certain contempt for language, we could all speak.

GOTTLIEB. Well, I understand that! — But why do you make such a secret of it?

HINZE. In order to avoid responsibility; if we so-called dumb animals were afflicted with language, there would be no more joy in the world. What all doesn't a dog have to do and learn! And the horse! They're stupid animals to let their intelligence be known; they have to indulge their vanity. But we cats are still the freest species because with all our skill we know how to act so unskilled that man utterly gives up training

GOTTLIEB. But why are you revealing all this to me?

HINZE. Because you are a good, a noble man, one of the few who finds no pleasure in servility and slavery;   that's why I reveal myself to you completely.

GOTTLIEB (gives him his hand). Excellent friend!

HINZE. Human beings delude themselves that the only remarkable thing about us is that instinctive murmuring sound which arises from a certain feeling of comfort; thus they often stroke us in an awkward way, and then we usually purr just to keep from being struck. If they knew the right way to treat us, believe me, they would be able to train our good nature to anything, and Michel, your neighbor's cat, would even be willing occasionally to jump through a hoop for the king.

GOTTLIEB. Of course you're right.

HINZE. I feel a tremendous love for you, Gottlieb. You have never stroked me the wrong way; you let me sleep when I wanted to; you objected whenever your brothers wanted to pick me up and take me out into the dark to see the so-called electrical sparks, — for all this I now want to show my gratitude.

GOTTLIEB. Noblehearted Hinze! Ha, how unjust they were to speak unkindly and contemptuously of you and to doubt your loyalty and devotion! My eyes are opened; how my knowledge of human nature has increased so unexpectedly!

FISCHER. Friends, what's happened to our hopes for a domestic drama?

LEUTNER. It's almost too insane.

SCHLOSSER. I think I'm dreaming.

HINZE. You're a fine man, Gottlieb, but — don't take this the wrong way — you're a little bit narrow-minded, you know — ignorant, not one of the best minds, if I may speak so freely.

GOTTLIEB. Oh God, it's true.

HINZE. For example, right now you don't know what to do next.

GOTTLIEB. You've read my mind.

HINZE. If you were to have a muff made from my fur . . .

GOTTLIEB. Don't hold it against me, dear friend, that earlier such a thought just passed through my mind.

HINZE. No, no, it was a very human thought. — Can you think of no way to support yourself?

GOTTLIEB. Nothing at all.

HINZE. You could carry me around and show me for money, — but that's not a secure way of life.

GOTTLIEB. No.

HINZE. You could publish a journal, or a German newspaper, with the motto "Homo sum"; or a novel — I could help you with it — but that is too much trouble.

GOTTLIEB. Yes.

HINZE. Well, I want to take ever better care of you; you can depend on it that through me you shall find success and happiness.

GOTTLIEB. O best, most noblehearted of men!

(He embraces him tenderly.)

HINZE. But you have to trust me.

GOTTLIEB. Absolutely — now that I know your honorable spirit.

HINZE. Well then, would you please bring in the shoemaker right away to measure me for a pair of boots.

GOTTLIEB. The shoemaker? — Boots?

HINZE. You're surprised; but to do what I intend to do for you I will have to walk and run so much that boots will be a necessity.

GOTTLIEB. But why not shoes?

HINZE. Gottlieb, you don't understand the matter; they have to lend me a dignity, an imposing air, in short, a certain manliness which one can never attain in shoes.

GOTTLIEB. Well, as you please — but the shoemaker will be surprised.

HINZE. Not at all, we just must not act as if it were anything special that I want to wear boots; people get used to anything.

GOTTLIEB. That's certainly true; in fact, it already seems perfectly natural for me to be having a conversation with you.— There goes the shoemaker now. — Hey! Pst! Mr. Leichdorn![2] Could I speak to you for a minute?

(The shoemaker enters.)

SHOEMAKER. Cheers! — What's new?

GOTTLIEB. You haven't done any work for me in a long time . . .

SHOEMAKER. No, my friend, actually I don't have much at all to do right now.

GOTTLIEB. I would like to have another pair of boots made.

SHOEMAKER. Please sit down; I have my measure with me.

GOTTLIEB. Not for me, but for my young friend there.

SHOEMAKER. For him? — Fine.

(HINZE sits down and extends his right leg.)

SHOEMAKER. How would you like them, sir?

HINZE. First of all, good soles; then brown flaps; and, above all, stiff.

SHOEMAKER. Fine. — *(He measures.)* — Would you be so kind as to draw
in your claws — I mean nails — a bit? I've already scratched myself.
(He measures.)

HINZE. And they have to be ready quickly. *(Because his leg is being
stroked, he begins to purr involuntarily.)*

SHOEMAKER. The gentleman is really pleased.

GOTTLIEB. Yes, he's in high spirits; he's just come from school; — what
they call a sly dog.

SHOEMAKER. Well, 'bye now. *(Exit.)*

GOTTLIEB. Wouldn't you like to have your whiskers trimmed a little, too?

HINZE. Absolutely not. I look much more respectable as I am. And as you
must know, that causes us cats to lose our virility immediately. A cat
without whiskers is but a contemptible creature.

GOTTLIEB. If I only knew what you have in mind.

HINZE. You'll know soon enough. — I want to go for a little stroll on the
roofs now; there's a beautiful, open view up there; and you can
usually catch a pigeon too.

GOTTLIEB. As a good friend, I want to warn you not to get caught at it.

HINZE. Don't worry, I'm not a novice. — Good-bye for a while. *(Exit.)*

GOTTLIEB *(alone).* In natural history it always says that one can't trust cats, and that they belong to the lion family, and I have a dreadful fear of lions. Now if the cat had no conscience, he could run away with my boots for which I have to spend my last penny, and peddle them somewhere; or it's possible that he wants to make up to the shoemaker in order to find a job with him. — But he already has a cat. — No, Hinze, my brothers have betrayed me, so I'll take my chances with you. — He spoke so nobly, he was so touched, — there he sits up on the roof and cleans his whiskers, — forgive me, dear friend, that I could doubt your magnanimity for even a moment.

(He exits.)

FISCHER. What nonsense!

MÜLLER. Why does the cat need the boots? — So that he can walk better? — Stupid stuff!

SCHLOSSER. But it's as if I saw a cat in front of me!

LEUTNER. Quiet! The scene is changing!

[Scene 2]

(Hall in the royal palace. The King with crown and sceptre. The Princess, his daughter.)

KING. Already a thousand handsome princes, my precious daughter, have sought your hand and have laid their kingdoms at your feet, but you've paid no attention to any of them; tell us the reason, my jewel.

PRINCESS. My most gracious father, I have always thought that my heart would have to feel certain emotions before I would bend my neck under the yoke of marriage. For a marriage without love, so they say, is the true hell on earth.

KING. That's right, my dear daughter. Oh, indeed, indeed, you have spoken the truth: a hell on earth! Oh, if only I were not able to discuss it! I would rather have remained ignorant! But, my precious jewel, I could tell a tale about it, as they say. Your mother, my most blessed spouse, — oh, Princess, look, the tears come to my eyes even in my old age, — she was a good queen, she wore the crown with an indescribable majesty, — but she gave me little peace. — Oh well, may her ashes rest in peace alongside her royal relatives!

PRINCESS. His Majesty excites himself too much.

KING. When the memory of it comes back to me, — o my child, on my knees I beseech you, — be careful in marrying. It is a great truth that one mustn't buy linen and a bridegroom by candlelight; a truth which should be written in every book. — What I have suffered! No day passed without a quarrel! I couldn't sleep peacefully, I couldn't administer the affairs of the realm in peace, I couldn't think about anything, I couldn't read a book — I was always interrupted. And yet my spirit still yearns for you at times, immortal Klothilde. — My eyes smart, — I'm a regular old fool.

PRINCESS *(tenderly)*. My father!

KING. I tremble when I think of all the dangers which lie ahead of you; for even if you should fall in love now, my daughter — oh, you should just see what thick books wise men have filled on the subject — you see, your very passion can thus make you miserable again. The happiest, the most blissful feeling can ruin us; love is like a trick goblet — instead of nectar we often drink poison, then our pillow is wet with tears, all hope, all comfort is gone. *(A trumpet is heard.)* It can't be dinnertime already? Of course, another new prince who wants to fall in love with you. — Take care, my daughter, you are my only child, and you don't know how close to my heart your happiness lies.

(He kisses her and exits; applause is heard in the pit.)

FISCHER. Now there's a scene with some sound common sense.

SCHLOSSER. I'm also touched.

MÜLLER. He's an outstanding ruler.

FISCHER. He didn't really even need to appear with the crown.

SCHLOSSER. It completely destroys the sympathy which one has for him as a tender father.

THE PRINCESS (alone). I simply can't understand why none of the princes has yet awakened love in my heart. My father's warnings always stay in my mind; he is a great monarch and yet a good father too — if only his hasty temper didn't so often suddenly get the better of him. Thus, good luck and bad always come together. My happiness lies in the sciences and the arts; books are all my joy.

(The Princess; Leander, the Court Scholar.)

LEANDER. Well, your Royal Highness!

(They sit down.)

PRINCESS. Here is my composition; I've titled it "Night Thoughts."

LEANDER (reads). Excellent! Inspired! — Ah! It's as if I could hear the hour of midnight striking. When did you write it?

PRINCESS. Yesterday, after lunch.

LEANDER. Beautifully conceived! Truly beautifully conceived! — But, with your gracious permission: — "The moon shined sadly down upon the world," — if you will not take it amiss, it must read: "shone down."

PRINCESS. Very well, I'll make a note of it for the future. It's ridiculous that poetry writing is made so difficult; one can't put down five or six lines without making an error.

LEANDER. Yes, that's the obstinacy of language.

PRINCESS. Aren't the emotions tenderly and delicately expressed?

LEANDER. Indescribably! It's almost beyond comprehension, how a feminine brain could have written something like this!

PRINCESS. Now I think I should try my hand at moonlit scenes of nature. Don't you agree?

LEANDER. Inevitably, you go further and further, you're climbing higher and higher.

PRINCESS. I've also started a play: *The Unhappy Misanthrope; or: Lost Peace and Regained Innocence.*

LEANDER. The title alone is enchanting.

PRINCESS. And then I feel an incomprehensible urge within me to write some horrible ghost story. — As we said, if only it weren't for those grammatical errors!

LEANDER. Don't let that stop you, incomparable one, they can easily be corrected.

(Valet enters.)

VALET. The Prince of Malsinki, who has just arrived, wishes to pay his respects to Her Royal Highness. *(Exit.)*

LEANDER. Your obedient servant. *(Exit.)*

(Prince Nathaniel of Malsinki and the King enter.)

KING. Here, Prince, is my daughter, a young, simple thing, as you can see. *(Aside.)* Courteous, my daughter, polite, he is a distinguished prince, from far away, his country isn't even on my map; I've already looked; I have a tremendous respect for him.

PRINCESS. I am happy to have the pleasure of making your acquaintance.

NATHANIEL. Beautiful Princess, the report of your beauty has spread so far through the entire world that I have come here from a far distant corner to have the happiness of seeing you face to face.

KING. It's astonishing how many countries and kingdoms there are! You wouldn't believe how many thousand crown princes have already been here to court my daughter; they often arrive by the dozens, especially when the weather is nice, — and now you've come all the way . . . — pardon me, topography is quite an extensive science — in what area does your country lie?

NATHANIEL. Mighty King, if you travel from here, first take the great highway, then turn right and continue straight on; when you come to a mountain, turn left again, proceed to the ocean and sail directly north (if, of course, the wind is favorable); and thus you'll come, if the trip goes well, to my realm in a year and a half.

KING. By George! I'll have to have my court scholar explain that to me. — Then you're probably a neighbor of the North Pole, or Zodiac, or something like that?

NATHANIEL. Not that I was aware.

KING. Maybe somewhere near the savages?

NATHANIEL. I beg your pardon, all my subjects are very tame.

KING. But you must live unbelievably far away! I still can't quite grasp it.

NATHANIEL. There is as yet no exact geography of my country; I expect to discover more every day, and so it could easily turn out that we will actually be neighbors.

KING. That would be superb! And if it turns out a couple of countries still stand in our way, I will help you with your discoveries. Actually my neighbor is not a good friend of mine and he has a superb country. All our raisins come from there; I would be only too glad to have it. — But one other thing: tell me, since you live so far away, how are you able to speak our language so fluently?

NATHANIEL. Hush!

KING. What?

NATHANIEL. Hush! Hush!

KING. I don't understand.

NATHANIEL (softly to him). Keep quiet about it; otherwise the audience down there is going to notice that that's very unnatural.

KING. It doesn't matter; the audience was applauding before, so I've still got them under control.

NATHANIEL. You see, it's only for the sake of the drama that I speak your language; otherwise it would be incomprehensible.

KING. Ah! Yes, of course. Well, come along, Prince, the table is set!

(The Prince escorts the Princess out; the King leads the way.)

FISCHER. What damnable improbabilities there are in this play!

SCHLOSSER. And the king doesn't remain at all true to his character.

LEUTNER. Plays should always remain perfectly true to Nature. Why can't the Prince speak a completely foreign language and have an interpreter translate it? Why doesn't the Princess make a grammatical error once in a while since she herself admits that she writes incorrectly?

MÜLLER. Of course! Of course! — The entire thing is utter nonsense; the author himself is always forgetting what he has said the moment before.

[Scene 3]

(In front of a tavern. Lorenz, Kunz, Michel are sitting on a bench.)

LORENZ. I will have to be going soon; it's still a long way home.

INNKEEPER. You're a subject of the king?

LORENZ. Yes. — What do you call your ruler?

INNKEEPER. He's just called Bogey.

LORENZ. That's a foolish title. Doesn't he have any other name?

INNKEEPER. When he has edicts issued, they always read: for the good of the public, the LAW demands. — So I think that's his real name: all petitions too are always submitted to the Law. He is a fearsome man.

LORENZ. I prefer to be under a king; a king is more dignified. They say the Bogey is a very merciless master.

INNKEEPER. He isn't especially merciful, that's true, but he is, on the other hand, justice itself; often cases are even sent to him from abroad, and he has to settle them.

LORENZ. Miraculous things are told about him; he is said to be able to change himself into any animal.

INNKEEPER. It's true, and he often goes around incognito and investigates the sentiments of his subjects; therefore we never trust a cat, or a strange dog or horse, because we always think our ruler could be hiding inside.

LORENZ. We have a better time of it there too; our king never goes out without putting on his crown, cloak and sceptre, so he is recognizable even a thousand yards away. — Well, take care! *(Exits.)*

INNKEEPER. Now he's already in his own country.

KUNZ. Is the border so near?

INNKEEPER. Of course, even that tree belongs to the king; from here you can see everything that happens in his country. The border here is my fortune; I would have been bankrupt long ago if the deserters from over there hadn't kept me going; several come almost every day.

MICHEL. Is service so hard there?

INNKEEPER. Not that, but running away is so easy, and simply because it's so strictly forbidden those fellows get a tremendous urge to desert. — Look, I bet that's another one coming!

(A Soldier comes running.)

SOLDIER. A mug of beer, Innkeeper! Quick!

INNKEEPER. Who are you?

SOLDIER. A deserter.

MICHEL. Perhaps out of "Filial Piety," like the play; the poor man, do take care of him, Innkeeper.

INNKEEPER. Why, if he has money, he won't be without beer.

(Goes into the tavern. Two Hussars come riding and dismount.)

FIRST HUSSAR. Thank God, we've gotten so far. — Your health, neighbor.

SOLDIER. This is the border.

SECOND HUSSAR. Yes, thank Heaven, — didn't we have to ride because of that fellow — beer, Innkeeper!

INNKEEPER *(with several glasses).* Here, gentlemen, a nice, cool drink; all three of you are pretty warm.

FIRST HUSSAR. Here, rascal! to your health!

SOLDIER. Many thanks; I'll hold your horses for you.

SECOND HUSSAR. The fellow can certainly run! It's good that the border isn't very far away, otherwise this would be a miserable assignment.

FIRST HUSSAR. Well, we have to be getting back. Adieu, deserter! Good luck on your way!

(They mount their horses and ride away.)

INNKEEPER. Are you going to stay here?

SOLIDER. No, I'm leaving; I have to enlist with the neighboring duke.

INNKEEPER. Stop and say hello next time you desert.

SOLDIER. Certainly. — Farewell. —

(They shake hands; the Soldier and the guest leave; the Innkeeper goes into the tavern. The curtain falls.)

Interlude

FISCHER. It's becoming more and more insane. — Now what was the purpose of the last scene?

LEUTNER. No purpose, it's completely superfluous; merely to bring in some new nonsense. The cat is completely lost from sight and there's absolutely no fixed point of view.

SCHLOSSER. I feel exactly as if I were drunk.

MÜLLER. In what period is the play supposed to be taking place? Hussars are a recent invention.

SCHLOSSER. We shouldn't put up with it; we should start stamping. We haven't the least idea what's happening in the play.

FISCHER. And no love, either! There's nothing in it for the heart, for the imagination!

LEUTNER. As for me, the next time anything else insane happens, I'm going to start stamping.

WIESENER *(to his neighbor)*. I like the play now.

NEIGHBOR. Very nice, very nice indeed; a great man, the author — he has imitated "The Magic Flute" well.

WIESENER. I liked the Hussars best. People seldom dare to bring horses onto the stage — but why not? They often have more sense than human beings. I would rather see a good horse than many of the human beings in modern plays.

NEIGHBOR. The Moors in Kotzebue — after all, a horse is nothing but another kind of Moor.

WIESENER. Do you know to which regiment the hussars belonged?

NEIGHBOR. I didn't even look at them carefully. Too bad that they went away so soon; I would like to see an entire play with nothing but hussars, — I like the cavalry so much.

LEUTNER *(to Botticher)*. What do you think of it all?

BOTTICHER. I can't stop thinking about the magnificent acting of the man who's playing the cat. What a study! What subtlety! What observation! What a costume!

SCHLOSSER. It's true; he actually looks like a large cat.

BOTTICHER. And just notice his entire mask — that's what I would call his costume; he has changed his natural appearance so entirely, this is a better term. Blessings on the ancients, in this respect! You probably don't know that the ancients played all roles without exception in masks, as you will find in Athenaeus, Pollux and others. It's difficult, you know, to have such an exact knowledge of all these things, because one has to look up the books oneself. Afterwards, though, one has the advantage of being able to quote them. There is a difficult passage in Pausanius —

FISCHER. You were going to be so kind as to discuss the cat.

BOTTICHER. Yes, of course. — I intended all I've been saying only parenthetically, so I most earnestly beg you to consider it as a footnote; and — to return to the cat: did you notice that he's not one of those black cats? No, on the contrary, he is almost entirely white and has only a few black spots; that's a magnificent expression of his good nature. In his fur one can already immediately foresee the action of the entire play and all the emotions it's supposed to arouse.

LEUTNER. That's true.

FISCHER. The curtain is going up again!

ACT II

[Scene 1]

(Room in a peasant hut.)

(Gottlieb, Hinze. Both are sitting at a small table and eating.)

GOTTLIEB. Did you like it?

HINZE. Very good, very nice.

GOTTLIEB. But now my fate has to be determined soon, because otherwise I don't know what I ought to do.

HINZE. Just be patient another few days; good fortune takes a little time to grow. Besides, who would want to become happy all of a sudden? That happens only in books, my good man; things don't happen so fast in the real world.

FISCHER. Now just listen to that! The cat has the nerve to talk about the real world. — I'm about ready to go home; I'm afraid I'm going mad.

LEUTNER. It's almost as if that were what the author intended.

MÜLLER. An excellent esthetic pleasure, to be mad, I must admit!

GOTTLIEB. If I only knew, my dear Hinze, how you got so much experience, such intelligence.

HINZE. Do you really think that one lies for days by the stove and keeps one's eyes shut tight for nothing? I always went on studying there in silence. Secretly and unnoticed the power of reason grows; that's why one has made the least progress when one keeps longing to crane one's neck to look back at the ground one has already covered. — Now would you mind untying my napkin?

GOTTLIEB *(does it)*. A blessing on our meal! *(They kiss.)* Be satisfied with that.

HINZE. Thanks, from the bottom of my heart.

GOTTLIEB. The boots fit quite nicely, and you have a charming little foot.

HINZE. That's simply because we always walk on our toes, as you have probably read in your natural history.

GOTTLIEB. I have a great respect for you, — because of the boots.

HINZE *(hangs a knapsack around his neck)*. I'll be going now. — You see, I've also made myself a sack with a drawstring.

GOTTLIEB. What's it all for?

HINZE. Just leave it to me. I want to look like a hunter. — Where is my cane?

GOTTLIEB. Here.

HINZE. Well, good-bye. *(Exits.)*

GOTTLIEB. A hunter? — I just can't understand the man. *(Exits.)*

[Scene 2]

(Open field.)

HINZE *(with cane, knapsack and sack)* Splendid weather! — Later I'll have to lie down in the sun for a while. — *(He spreads out his sack.)* Now, Fortune, be with me! — I almost lose all my courage when I stop and consider that this capricious goddess so seldom favors shrewdly laid plans, that she always ends up by putting to shame the rationality of mortals. But, be calm, my heart, a kingdom is worth the effort of working and sweating a little! — If only there are no dogs here in the vicinity. I can't stand to look at the creatures; they are a race I despise because they so willingly submit to the lowliest servitude to men. They can't do anything but fawn and bite. They're utterly without manners, which are so important in society. — There's nothing to be caught. — *(He begins to sing a hunting song: "I slip through the field so still and wild, etc."; a nightingale in a nearby bush begins to warble.)* She sings wonderfully, the songstress of the grove. — How delicious she must taste! — The great of the earth are truly fortunate that they can eat nightingales and larks, as many as they like; we poor common people must content ourselves with the singing, with beautiful nature, with incomprehensibly sweet harmony. — It's unfortunate that I can't hear anything singing without wanting to eat it. — Nature! Nature! Why do you always disturb me in my tenderest emotions by having made me this way? — I almost feel like taking off my boots and sneaking up that tree; she must be sitting there. — *(Stamping in the pit.)* The nightingale has a good nature not to let herself be disturbed even by this martial music. She must taste delicious. These sweet dreams are making me forget my hunting. — There really is nothing to be caught. — Who's coming there?

(Two Lovers enter.)

HE. Do you hear the nightingale, my sweet life?

SHE. I'm not deaf, my dear.

HE. How my heart overflows with delight when I see all of harmonious nature gathered around me thus, when every sound only repeats the confession of my love, when the entire sky bends down to shower its ether down upon me.

SHE. You're raving, my love.

HE. Don't call the most natural feelings of my heart "raving." *(He kneels down.)* You see, I swear to you here in the sight of the glorious heavens!

HINZE *(politely stepping forward)*. I beg your pardon, but would you please be so kind as to go somewhere else? You're disturbing a hunt here with your lovely harmony.

HE. The sun be my witness, the earth, — and whatever else? You yourself, dearer to me than the earth, the sun and all the elements.— What do you want, my friend?

HINZE. The hunt, — I ask most humbly.

HE. Barbarian, who are you that dares to interrupt the oaths of love? You are not born of woman, you don't deserve the name of man!

HINZE. If you would only consider —

SHE. Just wait for a moment, sir; you can see that my lover, lost in intoxication, is down on his knees.

HE. Do you believe me now?

SHE. Didn't I already believe you, even before you had spoken a word?— *(She bends down to him lovingly.)* Dearest! — I — love you!— oh, inexpressibly.

HE. Am I mad? — Oh, and if I'm not mad, why don't I immediately go mad, miserable, wretched man that I am — from excessive joy? — I am no longer on the earth; look at me carefully, oh my dearest, and tell me whether I'm not perhaps standing in the sun?

SHE. You are in my arms, and they will never let you go again.

HE. Oh come, this open field is too confining for my emotions, we must climb the highest mountain to tell all of nature how happy we are! —

(They exit quickly and delightedly. Loud applause and calls of "Bravo" in the pit.)

WIESENER *(applauding).* The lover really went all out. Oh Lord, I clapped so hard, my hand has swollen up.

NEIGHBOR. When you're happy, you let yourself go!

WIESENER. Yes, that's the way I always am.

FISCHER. Ah! — Now there was something for the heart! — It makes you feel good again!

LEUTNER. Truly beautiful diction in that scene.

MÜLLER. But I wonder whether it is essential to the whole?

SCHLOSSER. I never worry about the whole: When I cry, I cry, and that's good enough; it was a divine passage.

HINZE. Such infatuated folk are some good in the world after all! They've all fallen back into a poetical mood out there, and the stamping has stopped. — There's nothing to be caught. — *(A rabbit creeps into the sack, he rushes over and draws the string.)* You see, my friend! A bit of game that's sort of a cousin of mine. Yes, that's the way of the world today, relative against relative, brother against brother. If one is to make his own way in the world, one must push others out of the way. — *(He takes the rabbit out the sack and puts it in his knapsack.)* Whoa! Whoa! — I really must be careful not to eat the game myself. I've got to tie up my knapsack quickly to curb my passions. — Bah! shame on you, Hinze! — Isn't it the duty of the noble soul to sacrifice himself and his inclinations for the happiness of his fellow creatures? That's the purpose for which we have our being, and he who can't do it, — oh, it were better for him had he never been born!

(He is about to exit; the audience applauds violently and cries "Encore." He has to speak the last beautiful passage again, then he bows respectfully and exits with the rabbit.)

FISCHER. Oh, what a noble man!

MÜLLER. What a beautiful human spirit!

SCHLOSSER. It's still possible to improve oneself by things like this. — But when I see such foolishness I would like to smash it.

LEUTNER. I also became very melancholy, — the nightingale, — the lovers, — the last tirade, — the play does have some truly beautiful passages!

[Scene 3]

(Hall in the palace. Large group of people. The King, the Princess, Prince Nathaniel, the Cook in full dress.)

KING *(sitting on the throne)*. Here, Cook, it's time for speaking and answering; I want to investigate the matter myself.

COOK *(going down on one knee)*. May it please Your Majesty to express Your commands for Your most faithful servant?

KING. One cannot do enough, my friends, to insure that a king, on whose shoulders rests the welfare of an entire country and innumerable subjects, should always remain in a good mood. For, should he get into a bad mood, he all too easily becomes a tyrant, a monster. For a good mood promotes cheerfulness, and cheerfulness, according to the observations of all the philosophers, makes man good; on the other hand, melancholy is thus to be regarded as a vice because it promotes all the vices. Who, I now ask, is most capable, in whose power is it to promote the good mood of a monarch, if not in the hands of a cook? — Are rabbits not very innocent animals? My favorite dish! — By means of these tender little animals I could manage never to tire of making my country happy, — and these rabbits he fails to provide! — Suckling pigs, every day, suckling pigs, — villain, I have finally had enough of it.

COOK. May my king not condemn me unheard. As Heaven is my witness, I've made every effort to find those cute little white animals. I have tried to buy them at any price, but they're absolutely not to be had. Do you think You would have such reason to doubt the love of Your subjects if even one of these rabbits were to be had?

KING. Enough of these rascally words; get to the kitchen and prove by your deeds that you love your king. — *(The cook exits.)* — Now I turn to you, my Prince, — and to you, my daughter. — I've learned, worthy Prince, that my daughter doesn't love you, that she can't love you. She is a thoughtless, irrational girl, but I give her credit for enough intelligence to have her reasons. — She brings me worry and grief, sorrow and concern, and my old eyes frequently overflow with tears when I think about what will happen to her after my death. — "You will be an old maid!" I've told her a thousand times. Seize your opportunity while it's still offered to you! But she won't listen. Well then, she will have to learn to feel.

PRINCESS. My Father, —

KING *(weeping and sobbing).* Go, ungrateful, disobedient girl. — By your refusal you are preparing an, ah!, all-too-early grave for my old gray head! *(He supports himself on the throne, covers his face with his cloak and weeps violently.)*

FISCHER. The king doesn't stay true to his character for even a moment.

(A Valet enters.)

VALET. Your Majesty, a strange man is outside and begs to be admitted to Your Majesty.

KING *(sobbing)*. Who is it?

VALET. Forgive me, my king, but I can't answer your question. Judging by his long white whiskers he should be an old man, and his face entirely covered with hair would almost confirm one in this opinion, but then again he has such lively, youthful eyes, such a strong, supple back, that one doesn't know what to make of him. He appears to be a wealthy man, for he's wearing a pair of magnificent boots, and as far as I can determine from his appearance he seems to be a hunter.

KING. Bring him in; I'm curious to see him.

(Valet exits and returns immediately with Hinze.)

HINZE. With Your Majesty's most gracious permission the Count of Carabas takes the liberty of presenting you with a rabbit.

KING *(delighted)*. A rabbit? — Do you hear that, people? — Oh, Fate has been reconciled with me again! — A rabbit?

HINZE *(takes it out of his knapsack)*. Here, great monarch.

KING. Here, — hold my scepter for a minute, Prince, — *(He feels the rabbit.)* fat! nicely fat! — From the Count of —

HINZE. Carabas.

KING. My, he must be an excellent man; I must get to know the man better. —Who is the man? Who of you knows him? —Why does he keep himself hidden? If such as he are idling about, what a loss for my land! I could cry for joy; *sends me a rabbit!* Valet, give it to the cook without delay.

(Valet takes it and exits.)

NATHANIEL. My king, I most humbly bid you farewell.

KING. Oh, yes, in my joy I had almost forgotten. — Farewell, Prince. Yes, you must make room for other suitors; there is no other way. —

Adieu! I wish you had a highway all the way home.

(Nathaniel kisses his hand and exits.)

KING *(shouting).* People! — Have my historian come!

(The Historian appears.)

KING. Here, friend, here's some material for our history of the world. — You do have your book with you?

HISTORIAN. Yes, my king.

KING. Then enter that on such and such a day (whatever the date is today) the Count of Carabas presented me with a very delicious rabbit.

(Historian sits down and writes.)

KING. Don't forget, *anno currentis.* — I have to think of everything, otherwise it's always done wrong. *(A trumpet is heard.)* — Ah, the dinner is ready. — Come, my daughter, don't cry; if it's not the Prince, it will be someone else. — Hunter, we thank you for your trouble; will you accompany us to the dining hall?

(They exit. Hinze follows.)

LEUTNER. I can't take much more of this! Where is the father who at first was so tender with his daughter and touched all of us so?

FISCHER. The only thing that bothers me is that not a person in the play is amazed at the cat; the king and everyone else acts as if it is just as it ought to be.

SCHLOSSER. My whole head is spinning from this strange stuff.

[Scene 4]

(Royal dining hall. Large table set for dinner. Accompanied by drums and trumpets enter: the King, the Princess, Leander, Hinze, several distinguished guests and Hanswurst,[3] and Servants who wait at the table.)

KING. Let's sit down, otherwise the soup will get cold. — Is the hunter taken care of?

A SERVANT. Yes, Your Majesty; he will eat with the clown here at the little table.

HANSWURST *(to Hinze)*. Let's sit down, otherwise the soup will get cold.

HINZE *(sits down)*. With whom have I the honor of dining?

HANSWURST. A man is what he is, Hunter, we can't all do the same thing. I'm a poor, exiled fugitive, a man who once a long time ago was amusing, who then later was thought to be stupid, tasteless and indecent, and who has now taken up service again in a strange land where he is again for a while thought to be amusing.

HINZE. What country do you come from?

HANSWURST. Just Germany, unfortunately. At a certain time my countrymen became so intelligent that they forbade all merriment on pain of punishment. Wherever I was seen, I was called unbearable names, such as tasteless, vulgar, bizarre — whoever laughed at me was persecuted just as I was, and thus I had to go into exile.

HINZE. Poor man!

HANSWURST. There are strange occupations in the world, Hunter; cooks live from appetites, tailors from vanity, and I from people's laughter; if they no longer laugh, then I must starve.

(Murmuring in the pit: a clown! a Hanswurst!)

HINZE. I don't care for any of the vegetable.

HANSWURST. Why? Don't be ridiculous, dig in.

HINZE. I can't bear white cabbage, I tell you.

HANSWURST. It will taste all the better to me. — Give me your hand; I have to get to know you better, Hunter.

HINZE. Here.

HANSWURST. Take the hand of a staunch, solid German; unlike so many of my countrymen, I'm not ashamed of being a German.

(He presses the cat's hand very tightly.)

HINZE. Ow! Ow!

(He resists, growls and scratches the jester.)

HANSWURST. Oh, ouch! Hunter! Are you possessed by the devil? — *(he stands up and goes weeping to the king.)* Your Majesty, the Hunter is a treacherous man; just look at the souvenir of his five fingers that he's left on me.

KING *(eating)*. Strange, — well, sit down again; in the future wear gloves if you want to be friends with him.

HANSWURST. A person has to watch out for you.

HINZE. Why did you squeeze me like that? Your staunch solidity be hanged!

HANSWURST. You scratch like a cat.

(Hinze laughs maliciously.)

KING. But what's wrong today? Why isn't there any intelligent conversation at the table? I don't enjoy a single bite, if my mind doesn't have some nourishment too. — Court Scholar, did you fall on your head today?

LEANDER *(eating)*. May it please Your Majesty —

KING. How far is the sun from the earth?

LEANDER. Two million four hundred thousand and seventy-one miles.

KING. And the orbit which the planets traverse?

LEANDER. A hundred thousand million miles.

KING. A hundred thousand million! — There's nothing in the world I like better to hear than such large numbers, — millions, trillions, — now there's something to think about. — But it's really a little much for me, a thousand million.

LEANDER. The human mind grows with the numbers.

KING. Tell me, how large is the whole world in its entirety — fixed stars, milky ways, nebulae, and all that stuff put together?

LEANDER. It can't even be expressed.

KING. You had better express it, or — *(threatening him with the scepter.)*

LEANDER. If we regard a million as one, then approximately ten times a hundred thousand trillions of such units which in themselves represent a million miles.

KING. Just think, children, think! — Would one have thought that the world could be so big? How that occupies the mind!

HANSWURST. Your Majesty, this bowl of rice here seems to me much more sublime.

KING. How's that, fool?

HANSWURST. With such enormous numbers one can't think at all, since the highest number again becomes in the end the smallest. All you need to do is think of all the numbers that are possible. As for me, I can never count above five.

KING. There's some truth in that. Scholar, — how many numbers are there then?

LEANDER. Infinitely many.

KING. Tell me quickly the highest number.

LEANDER. There is no highest, because a new number can always be added to the highest; the human mind has no limits here.

KING. The human mind is truly a marvelous thing.

HINZE. You must get fed up with being a fool here.

HANSWURST. One can't come up with anything new; there are already too
many working in this field.

LEANDER. The fool, my King, can never comprehend such things; I am
amazed moreover that Your Majesty is still amused by his tasteless
notions. Even in Germany they grew tired of him, and here in Utopia
you have taken him up, when thousands of wonderful and clever
amusements are available to us. He should be dismissed immediately,
for he only gives your good taste a bad name.

KING (throws the scepter at his head). Smart-aleck scholar! What
presumptuousness! What has gotten into you today? The fool pleases
me, me, his King, and if I find him in good taste how dare you say that
he is in bad taste? You're the court scholar and he the court jester.
You are both employed by me; the only difference is that he eats at
the little table with the foreign hunter. The fool does nonsensical
things at the table and you conduct rational discussions at the table;
both are supposed to while away my time and make the meal taste
good to me; where's the great difference then? — And then it does us
good to see a fool who is stupider than we are, who doesn't have our
gifts; one feels superior and is grateful to heaven. On that account
alone a stupid man is a pleasant companion for me. —

(The Cook serves the rabbit and leaves.)

KING. The rabbit! — I don't know, — the other gentlemen probably don't
care for it? —

(All bow.)

Well then, with your permission, I'll keep it for myself. —

(He eats.)

PRINCESS. The king seems to be making faces as if he were having one of
his attacks again.

KING (rising in a rage). The rabbit is burned! — Oh, Earth! — Oh pain!
What holds me back from sending the Cook most speedily to Hell!

PRINCESS. My father —

KING. How has this stranger wandered amongst men? His eyes are dry![4]

(All rise apprehensively, Hanswurst runs busily back· and forth, Hinze remains seated and stealthily eats.)

KING. A long, long good night! No rosy morn will ever break upon it!

PRINCESS. Quickly, someone bring the Soother.

KING. Let "Cook Philipp" be Hell's victory cry, each time it burns another thankless wretch!

PRINCESS. Where can the musician be?

KING. To be or not to be . . .

(The Soother enters with a Glockenspiel which he immediately plays.)

KING. What's wrong with me? *(Weeping.)* Ah, I've had another attack already. — Take the rabbit out of my sight. —

(Grief-stricken he lays his head on the table and sobs.)

A COURTIER. His Majesty suffers much.

(There arises a tremendous stamping and whistling in the pit; there is coughing and hissing, laughing in the balcony. The King gets up, arranges his cloak and sits down very majestically with his scepter. It is all in vain; the noise increases; all the actors forget their roles, a terrible pause on the stage. — Hinze has climbed onto a pillar. Dismayed, the Author comes onto the stage.)

AUTHOR. Gentlemen — most honorable public, — just a few words.

IN THE PIT. Quiet! quiet! the fool wants to speak.

AUTHOR. For Heaven's sake, don't disgrace me; the act is almost over. — Just look, the king is calm again; take an example from this great soul, who certainly has more cause than you to be beside himself.

FISCHER. More than we?

WIESENER *(to his neighbor).* But why are you stamping? We both like the play.

NEIGHBOR. Say, that's true, — absentmindedly, because everyone is doing it. *(Applauds as hard as he can.)*

AUTHOR. A few voices are still in my favor. Let my poor play please you, out of pity; only a rascal can give more than he has. Anyway, it'll soon be over, — I'm so confused and frightened that I don't know what else to tell you.

ALL. We don't want to hear anything, know anything.

AUTHOR *(angrily pulls the Soother forward).* The King is soothed; now soothe this raging flood too, if you can! *(Rushes off, beside himself. The Soother plays the bells, the stamping takes up the beat. He makes a sign: Apes and Bears appear and dance amiably around him; Eagles and other Birds; an Eagle sits on Hinze's head who is very frightened; two Elephants and two Lions dance along.)*

BALLET AND SINGING.[5]

THE FOUR-FOOTED ANIMALS. That sounds so splendid.

THE BIRDS. That sounds so beautiful.

UNITED CHORUS. I've never heard or seen anything like it.

(With this all those present dance an artistic quadrille; the King and his household are taken into the middle, Hinze and Hanswurst not excepted; general applause. Laughter. People stand up in the pit in order to see better; a few hats fall down from the balcony.)

THE SOOTHER *(sings during the ballet and the general pleasure of the audience).*

> *If all good men could find*
> *Such pretty bells as these,*
> *The foes of human kind*
> *Would vanish like a breeze;*
> *And men would all live free*
> *In lovely harmony.*

(The curtain falls; everyone shouts and applauds; the ballet is still heard for a while.)

Interlude

WIESENER. Splendid! Splendid!

NEIGHBOR. Now that's what I call a heroic ballet.

WIESENER. And so beautifully woven into the main plot.

LEUTNER. Beautiful music!

FISCHER. Divine!

SCHLOSSER. The ballet saved the play.

BOTTICHER. I still admire the acting of the cat. — By such details one recognizes the great and polished actor. For example, whenever he took the rabbit out of the sack, he lifted it each time by the ears, — that wasn't written down for him; did you notice how the king held it by the body? But you hold these animals by the ears because they can best stand it there. That's what I call a master!

MÜLLER. That's nicely analyzed.

FISCHER *(aside)*. He deserves to be taken by the ears himself for it.

BOTTICHER. And the fear when the eagle sat on his head! How, out of terror, he didn't even move, didn't even stir, — no description can express such perfected artistry.

MÜLLER. You go into it very deeply.

BOTTICHER. I flatter myself to be something of a connoisseur; of course that is not the case with all of you, and therefore one has to elucidate it to you a bit.

FISCHER. You are going to a lot of trouble.

BOTTICHER. Oh, when one loves art as much as I, it's a pleasant trouble. — A very shrewd thought has just occurred to me about the boots of the cat, and I admire the genius of the actor in it. — You see, at the beginning he's a cat; therefore he has to take off his natural clothing in order to assume the mask suitable for a cat. Now he's supposed to look just like a hunter (I deduce this from the fact that everyone calls him that, also no one wonders about him). An unskilled actor would certainly have put on a complete hunting outfit: — but — what would have happened to our illusion? We would perhaps have forgotten that he is basically a cat, and how uncomfortable for the actor would be a new outfit over the fur he already had on. With the boots however he just very skillfully suggests the hunter's outfit, and that such suggestions are completely satisfying aesthetically was well proven to us by the ancients who often —

FISCHER. Quiet! The third act is beginning. —

ACT III

(Room in a peasant hut. The Author, the Machinist.)

MACHINIST. Do you really think that will help?

AUTHOR. I beg you, I entreat you, don't refuse my request; my last hope
depends on it.

LEUTNER. Now what's this? — What are these men doing in Gottlieb's room?

SCHLOSSER. I'm not going to trouble my head about it any more.

MACHINIST. But, my dear friend, you're truly asking too much that all
that should be done in such a hurry, so on the spur of the moment.

AUTHOR. I think you're persecuting me too; you're enjoying my misfortune,
just like the others.

MACHINIST. Not in the least.

AUTHOR *(falls down before him)*. Then prove it by granting my request. If
the displeasure of the audience erupts again so loudly, then set all
your machines in motion when I signal to you! The second act ended
so differently than in my manuscript.

MACHINIST. What's this? — Who raised the curtain?

AUTHOR. Misfortune is pouring down on me; I'm lost! — *(Embarrassed,
he flees behind the scenes.)*

MACHINIST. There's never been an evening of such confusion. *(Exits. —
A pause.)*

WIESENER. Is that part of the play?

NEIGHBOR. Naturally; it motivates the transformations that follow.

FISCHER. This evening really should be written up in the theater almanac.

KING *(behind the scenes)*. No, I'm not going out, I won't do it. I can't stand
being laughed at.

AUTHOR. But you — dearest friend — it can't be changed.

HANSWURST. Well, I'll try my luck. *(He steps forward and bows comically toward the audience.)*

MÜLLER. Now what's the jester doing in the peasant cottage?

SCHLOSSER. I'm sure he wants to deliver a tasteless monologue.

HANSWURST. Forgive my boldness in saying a few words that don't actually belong in the play.

FISCHER. Oh, you should just keep quiet altogether; we don't even like you in the play, much less now that —

SCHLOSSER. A jester dares to talk to us?

HANSWURST. Why not? If I am laughed at, it doesn't bother me; in fact, it's my most ardent desire that you should laugh at me. So don't be embarrassed.

LEUTNER. That's pretty comical.

HANSWURST. What is admittedly rather unsuitable for the King is all the more fitting for me; therefore he didn't want to appear, but rather left this important announcement to me.

MÜLLER. But we don't want to hear anything.

HANSWURST. My dear German countrymen —

SCHLOSSER. I believe the play is set in Asia?

HANSWURST. But now, you see, now I'm speaking to you merely as an actor to the audience.

SCHLOSSER. Folks, I've had it! My mind is snapping.

HANSWURST. Please be advised that the preceding scene, which you just saw, doesn't belong in the play at all.

FISCHER. Doesn't belong? What was it doing there then?

HANSWURST. The curtain was raised too soon. It was a private conversation that wouldn't have taken place on stage at all if there had been a little more room behind the scenes. So if you entered into the illusion it's really so much the worse; anyway, now be so good as to erase the error from your minds. Beginning now — please try to understand me, from the moment I leave the stage — only then will the third act begin. Just between us: all the preceding had nothing to do with anything. But you are to be compensated; for a change, a lot of things will soon be coming up that are quite relevant. I have spoken to the Author myself and he has promised me.

FISCHER. Yes, your author is just the man for it.

HANSWURST. He is good for nothing, isn't he? Well, I'm glad somebody else has my tastes.

THE BALCONY. Oh, we all do, we all do!

HANSWURST. Your obedient servant; you're too kind! — Yes, God knows, he's a miserable author, — to give only one bad example: what a wretched part he's given me! Where am I witty and funny? I appear in so few scenes, and I believe, if I hadn't appeared now because of a happy accident, I wouldn't have appeared again at all.

AUTHOR *(rushing forward)*. Shameless Wretch —

HANSWURST. You see! He's envious of even the small part I'm playing now.

AUTHOR *(on the other side of the stage, with a bow)*. Honorable people! I would never have dared give this man a larger part, for I know your taste —

HANSWURST (on the other side). *Your* taste! — Now you see the envy. — And you've all just declared that my taste is the same as yours!

AUTHOR. I wanted to prepare you beforehand, by means of the present play, for even more extravagant creations of the imagination.

ALL IN THE PIT. How? — What?

HANSWURST. No doubt for plays in which I'd have no part at all.

AUTHOR. Such an education, you know, can only proceed step-by-step.

HANSWURST. Don't believe a word he says!

AUTHOR. Now I'll take my leave so as not to interrupt the course of the
   play any longer. *(Exits.)*

HANSWURST. Adieu, gentlemen, until we meet again. — *(He exits, and
   returns quickly.)* By the way! another thing! — This which has just
   taken place between us is also not a part of the play. *(Exit.)*

   (The Pit laughs.)

HANSWURST *(returns quickly)*. Let us go on through the miserable play
   today; act as if you don't notice how bad it is, and as soon as I get
   home I'll sit down and write one for you that will surely please you.
   (Exit. Many applaud.)

[Scene 1]

(Gottlieb and Hinze enter.)

GOTTLIEB. My dear Hinze, it's true you're doing a lot for me, but I still
   can't see what good it's going to do me.

HINZE. On my word, I intend to make you happy.

GOTTLIEB. It has to happen soon, very soon, or else it will be too late; —
   it's already seven-thirty and the comedy is over at eight.

HINZE. What in the devil does that mean?

GOTTLIEB. Oh, I was just thinking! I meant to say, Look! how beautifully
   the sun has risen! — The damned prompter speaks so unclearly, and
   if you want to ad lib once in a while it always goes wrong.

HINZE *(softly)*. Pull yourself together, or the entire play is going to break
   into a thousand pieces.

SCHLOSSER. Somebody tell me — why can't I make sense out of anything
   anymore?

FISCHER. My mind's stopped working too!

GOTTLIEB. Then my fortune is to be decided today?

HINZE. Yes, dear Gottlieb, before the sun goes down. — Listen, my love for you is so great that I'd walk through fire for you, — and you doubt my sincerity?

WIESENER. Did you hear that? — He is going to walk through fire. — Beautiful! we're going to get the scene from the *Magic Flute,* with the water and fire.

NEIGHBOR. But cats don't go into the water.

WIESENER. So much the greater then is the cat's love for his master; you see, that's just what the author wants to make us understand.

HINZE. Now what would you like to make of yourself in the world?

GOTTLIEB. Oh, I can't even say.

HINZE. Would you like to become a prince or king, perhaps?

GOTTLIEB. That more than anything.

HINZE. Do you also feel the power within yourself to make a people happy?

GOTTLIEB. Why not? If only I'm happy first.

HINZE. Well then, be content; I swear to you, you shall ascend the throne. *(Exits.)*

GOTTLIEB. It would take a miracle. — But then so many things in the world come about unexpectedly. *(Exits.)*

BOTTICHER. Notice the infinite refinement with which the cat always holds his cane.

FISCHER. We've put up with you long enough; you're even more boring than the play.

SCHLOSSER. You've addled our brains more than anything else.

MÜLLER. You talk, talk, talk, and don't even know what you're talking about.

MANY VOICES. Out! Out! He's a nuisance! *(A crowd; Botticher finds himself forced to leave the theater.)*

FISCHER. Him and his refinement!

SCHLOSSER. He always annoyed me, he thought he was such a connoisseur.

[Scene 2]

(Open field.)

HINZE *(with knapsack and sack).* I've gotten quite used to hunting; every day I catch partridges, rabbits and such, and the dear little animals are becoming better and better trained at letting themselves be caught. — *(He spreads out his sack.)* The time for nightingales is past; I don't hear a single one singing.

(The Two Lovers enter.)

HE. Go away, you're a nuisance.

SHE. You make me sick.

HE. A fine romance!

SHE. Miserable hypocrite, how you deceived me!

HE. And what's happened to your infinite tenderness?

SHE. And your faithfulness?

HE. Your infatuation?

SHE. Your raptures?

BOTH. Gone to hell! that comes from marrying!

HINZE. The hunt has never been so disrupted. —Would you be so good as to notice that this open field is obviously too narrow for your sufferings, and go climb some mountain?

HE. Wretch! *(Boxes Hinze's ear.)*

SHE. Boor! *(Hits him from the other side.)*

HINZE *(growls).*

SHE. I think we should try a separation.

HE. I'm at your command. *(The Lovers exit.)*

HINZE. Nice folk, these so-called humans. — Look, two partridges, I'll grab them quickly. — Now, Fortune, be quick, I'm beginning to get bored. — I no longer have any desire to eat partridges. Thus it is clear that we, by mere habit, are able to instill in our natures all possible virtues. *(Exits.)*

[Scene 3]

(Hall in the palace. The King on his throne with the Princess, Leander at a rostrum, opposite him Hanswurst at another rostrum; in the middle of the hall a hat, which is inlaid with gold and decorated with colorful feathers, hangs upon a high pole; the entire court is assembled.)

KING. Never before has a man been of such great service to his country as this esteemed Count of Carabas. Our historian has already almost filled a thick volume, so often has he, through his hunter, presented me with dainty and delicious gifts, sometimes even twice in one day. My gratitude to him is boundless, and I desire nothing so earnestly as sometime to find an opportunity to repay something of my great debt to him.

PRINCESS. My dear father, would you not most graciously permit that the learned debate should now begin? My heart is yearning for this intellectual activity.

KING. Yes, it may now begin. — Court Scholar, — Court Fool, — You both know that the one of you who is victorious in the debate wins that expensive hat. I had it placed here so that you may always have it before your eyes and not be lacking in wit.

(Leander and Hanswurst bow.)

LEANDER. The thesis which I assert is that a newly published play, entitled *Puss in Boots,* is a good play.

HANSWURST. That is exactly what I deny.

LEANDER. Prove that it's bad.

HANSWURST. Prove that it's good.

LEUTNER. Now what's this? — they're talking about the very play that's being performed here, if I'm not mistaken.

MÜLLER. Exactly the same.

LEANDER. The play is, even if not entirely perfect, still praiseworthy in some respects.

HANSWURST. In absolutely no respect.

LEANDER. I maintain there is wit in it.

HANSWURST. I maintain there is none.

LEANDER. You're a fool, how can you pretend to judge wit?

HANSWURST. And you're a scholar; how can you pretend to understand wit?

LEANDER. Several characters are well developed.

HANSWURST. Not a one.

LEANDER. Yet, even if I concede everything else, the audience is well presented in it.

HANSWURST. An audience never has a character.

LEANDER. I'm almost astonished by this impertinence.

HANSWURST *(to the pit)*. Isn't he a foolish fellow? The honorable audience
and I are now like old friends, and sympathize in regard to taste, and
still he attempts to maintain, in opposition to my opinion, that the
audience in *Puss in Boots* is well presented.

FISCHER. The audience? No audience appears in the play.

HANSWURST. Even better! Then absolutely no audience appears in it?

MÜLLER. Why, not at all, unless he means the several kinds of fools that
appear.

HANSWURST. Now, you see, Scholar? What the gentlemen down there say
must certainly be true.

LEANDER. I'm getting confused, — but I still won't concede the victory
to you.

   (Hinze enters.)

HANSWURST. Hunter, a word!

   (Hinze approaches; Hanswurst speaks secretly with him.)

HINZE. If that's all it is. — *(He takes off his boots, climbs up the pole, takes
the hat, leaps down and puts the boots on again.)*

HANSWURST. Victory! Victory!

KING. By George! The hunter's really skillful!

LEANDER. I only regret that I've been defeated by a fool, that learning
must lower its sails before folly.

KING. Be quiet; you wanted to have the hat, he wanted to have the hat, so
again I see no difference. — But what have you brought, Hunter?

HINZE. The Count of Carabas sends his most humble respects to Your

Majesty and has taken the liberty of sending you these two partridges.

KING. Too much! Too much! I sink under the burden of my gratitude. I should long ago have done my duty and visited him; today I will procrastinate no longer. — Have my state carriage put in order, eight horses in front, I want to go for a ride with my daughter! — You, Hunter, are to show us the way to the castle of the Count. *(Exits with his retinue.)*

(Hinze, Hanswurst.)

HINZE. What was your debate about?

HANSWURST. I maintained that a certain play, which in fact I don't know at all, *Puss in Boots,* is a miserable play.

HINZE. Oh?

HANSWURST. Adieu, Hunter. *(Exit.)*

HINZE *(alone).* I'm so depressed! — I myself helped the fool to his victory against a play in which I'm acting the title role! — Fate! Fate! Into what entanglements you so often lead us mortals! But if only it should come about, if only I could succeed in placing my beloved Gottlieb on the throne, then I will gladly forget all my troubles. — The King wants to visit the Count? that's another bad situation I'll have to clear up. — The great important day has now come when I need you, you boots, above all! Now don't desert me, for everything must be decided today! *(Exits.)*

FISCHER. But just tell me how is it, — the play itself, — it's appearing again as a play in the play?

SCHLOSSER. Don't look now, but I've lost my mind. Didn't I tell you, though, that's just the esthetic pleasure one should have here?

LEUTNER. No tragedy has ever affected me like this farce.

[Scene 4]

(In front of the tavern.)

THE INNKEEPER *(reaping grain with a scythe).* That's hard work! — Oh well, people can't desert every day either; I just wish the harvest were over. Life consists of nothing but work; now tapping kegs, now washing glasses, now pouring drinks, now even reaping. Life means work. And now some scholars in their books are wicked enough to put sleep out of fashion, because we don't live right for the time. But I'm a great friend of sleep.

(Hinze enters.)

HINZE. Whoever wants to hear something wonderful, listen to me now. How I ran! First from the royal palace to Gottlieb; secondly with Gottlieb to the palace of the Bogey where I left him outside in the forest; thirdly from there back to the king; fourthly I'm now running ahead of the king's carriage like a courier and showing him the way. — Hey! good friend!

INNKEEPER. Who's there? — Countryman, you must be a stranger, because the people around here know I don't sell beer at this time; I need it for myself. Whoever does work like mine also needs to fortify himself; I'm sorry, but I can't help you.

HINZE. I don't want any beer; I never drink beer; I just want to say a few words to you.

INNKEEPER. You must be a real ne'er-do-well to attempt to disturb diligent people at their work.

HINZE. I don't want to disturb you. Just listen: the neighboring king is going to drive by here, perhaps he'll get out and inquire to whom these villages belong; if your life is dear to you, if you don't want to be hanged or burned, then answer this way: to the Count of Carabas.

INNKEEPER. But, Sir, we're subject to the Law.

HINZE. I know that; but, as I said, if you don't want to come to a sudden end, then this area belongs to the Count of Carabas. *(Exits.)*

INNKEEPER. Many thanks! — that would be a fine opportunity to escape all work; I would only have to tell the king that the country belongs to the Bogey. But no. An idle mind is the devil's workshop. *Ora et labora* is my motto.

(A beautiful coach with eight horses, many servants behind; the coach stops; the King and the Princess get out.)

PRINCESS. I feel a certain curiosity to see the Count.

KING. I do too, my daughter. — Good day, my friend! to whom do these villages here belong?

INNKEEPER *(to himself)*. He asked as if he wanted to have me hanged at once. — To the Count of Carabas, Your Majesty.

KING. A beautiful country. — I always thought that the country would have to look entirely different if I crossed the border, just the way it does on the map. — Help me a little. *(He quickly climbs a tree.)*

PRINCESS. What are you doing, my royal father?

KING. Out in beautiful nature I love open views.

PRINCESS. Can you see far?

KING. Oh yes, and if those cursed mountains weren't in the way, I could see even further. — Oh, ugh! the tree is full of caterpillars. *(He climbs down again.)*

PRINCESS. That's because it's nature which hasn't been idealized yet; imagination must first ennoble it.

KING. I wish you could get these caterpillars off me by means of your imagination. — But get in, we'll drive on.

PRINCESS. Farewell, good, innocent peasant. *(They get in, the coach drives on.)*

INNKEEPER. How the world has changed! — If you read in old books or hear old people tell it, you would always get pieces of gold or such-like if you spoke to a king or prince. In the old days such a king wouldn't even presume to open his mouth, if he hadn't first stuck some money into people's hands. But now! — How is a man supposed to find his fortune in an unexpected quarter, if it's no longer possible even with kings? — Innocent peasant! I wish to God I were innocent. — But that comes from the new sentimental portrayals of country life. Such a king is powerful but still envies our kind. — I just thank God that he didn't hang me. The strange hunter was after all our Bogey himself. — At least it'll now appear in the newspaper that the king spoke to me graciously. *(Exits.)*

[Scene 5]

(Another region.)

KUNZ *(who is reaping grain)*. Rough work! If I at least were doing it for myself — but this working for the court! You have to sweat for the Bogey and he doesn't even thank you for it. — It's always said in this world that laws are necessary in order to keep people in order, but I can't see why we need *our Law,* which is tearing us to pieces.

HINZE *(comes running)*. Now I have blisters on my feet already! — Well, it doesn't matter; Gottlieb, Gottlieb must get the throne as a result! — Hey! good friend!

KUNZ. What kind of fellow is that?

HINZE. The king is going to drive by here in just a minute; when he asks you who this belongs to you must answer, "to the Count of Carabas," or you'll be hacked up into a thousand million pieces. Such is the law, for the good of the public.

FISCHER. How's that? For the good of the public?

SCHLOSSER. Of course, because otherwise the play would have no ending.

HINZE. Your life is dear to you! *(Exits.)*

KUNZ. That's just how the edicts always sound. Well, it suits me fine to say that, as long as it doesn't mean new taxes. But a person can't always trust a new deal. *(The coach drives up and stops; King and Princess get out.)*

KING. Another beautiful stretch of country. We've been seeing a lot of really beautiful country. — To whom does the land here belong?

KUNZ. To the Count of Carabas.

KING. He has magnificent lands, it must be true, — and so near to mine. Daughter, he would be a good match for you. What do you think?

PRINCESS. You embarrass me, Father. — But what new things one sees when traveling. Tell me, good farmer, why are you cutting down that straw?

KUNZ *(laughing)*. That's the harvest, Mamsell Queen, the grain.

KING. The grain? — What do you use it for?

KUNZ *(laughing)*. Bread is baked from it.

KING. Now I ask you, daughter; for heaven's sake! — bread is baked from it! — Who would have thought it? — Nature is something truly wonderful. — Here, good friend, buy yourself a drink, it's warm today. — *(He climbs in again with the Princess; the coach drives on.)*

KUNZ. If he weren't a king, you would almost think he was stupid. Doesn't know what grain is! Well, you learn something new every day! And he did give me a shiny gold piece, and now I'm going to go have a tankard of good beer right away. *(Exits.)*

[Scene 6]

(Another region on a river.)

GOTTLIEB. I've been standing here for two hours now waiting for my friend Hinze. — He still hasn't come. — There he is! How he's running! He seems to be entirely out of breath.

HINZE *(comes running)*. Now, friend Gottlieb, quickly get undressed.

GOTTLIEB. Undressed?

HINZE. And then jump into the water here. —

GOTTLIEB. Into the water?

HINZE. And then I'll throw your clothes into the bushes. —

GOTTLIEB. Into the bushes?

HINZE. And then you're taken care of!

GOTTLIEB. I believe it; when I've drowned and my clothes are gone, I'll have been well taken care of.

HINZE. This is no time for joking —

GOTTLIEB. I'm not joking. Is this why I've had to wait here?

HINZE. Get undressed!

GOTTLIEB. Well, I'll do anything to please you.

HINZE. Come, you're just going to take a little swim. *(He exits with him and returns with the clothes which he throws into the bushes.)* — Help! Help! Help! *(The coach drives up; the King looks out the door.)*

KING. What's wrong, Hunter? Why are you shouting like that?

HINZE. Help, Your Majesty, the Count of Carabas has drowned.

KING. Drowned!

PRINCESS *(in the coach)*. Carabas!

KING. My daughter in a faint! — The Count drowned!

HINZE. Maybe he can still be saved; he's lying there in the water.

KING. Servants! do everything, anything, to save the noble man.

A SERVANT. We've saved him, Your Majesty.

HINZE. Misfortune after misfortune, my King. — The Count was bathing here in the clear stream and some rascal has stolen his clothes.

KING. Open my trunk immediately! Give him some of my clothes! — Cheer up, daughter, the Count has been saved.

HINZE. I have to hurry. *(Exits.)*

GOTTLIEB *(in the King's clothing)*. Your Majesty.

KING. It's the Count! I know him because of my clothes! — Get in, my good sir, — How are you? — Where do you get all the rabbits? — I can't get over my joy! — Drive on, coachman! — *(The coach drives off quickly.)*

A SERVANT. They move quick as the hangman — now I have the pleasure of following on foot, and besides I'm wet as a cat. *(Exits.)*

LEUTNER. How many more times is the coach going to appear!

WIESENER. Neighbor! — You're sleeping.

NEIGHBOR. Not at all, — a beautiful play!

[Scene 7]

(The Bogey's palace. The Bogey appears as a rhinoceros with a poor Peasant before him.)

PEASANT. May it please the honorable Bogey —

BOGEY. Justice must be done, my friend.

PEASANT. I can't pay quite yet —

BOGEY. But you lost the trial; the law demands money and your punishment;

therefore your property must be sold; there is no other way and justice must be done.

(Peasant exits.)

BOGEY *(who transforms himself into an ordinary Bogey again)*. The people would lose all respect if they weren't compelled this way through fear.

(With much bowing, a Magistrate enters.)

MAGISTRATE. May it please you, — gracious sire — I —

BOGEY. What's wrong with you, my friend?

MAGISTRATE. With your kindest permission I am trembling and quivering before your terrible countenance.

BOGEY. Oh, this is far from being my most horrible form.

MAGISTRATE. I actually came, — about matters, — in order to ask you to take my part against my neighbor, — I also brought this purse along, — but the countenance of the Law is too terrifying for me.

(Bogey suddenly transforms himself into a mouse and sits in a corner.)

MAGISTRATE. What's happened to the Bogey?

BOGEY *(in a small voice)*. Put the money on the table over there; I'm sitting here in order not to terrify you.

MAGISTRATE. Here. — *(Puts down the money.)* Oh, justice is a marvelous thing. — How can one be frightened by a mouse like that? *(Exits.)*

BOGEY *(assumes his natural form)*. A nice purse, — One also has to sympathize with human weaknesses.

(Hinze enters.)

HINZE. With your permission, — *(aside)* Hinze, you have to find courage, — Your Excellency —

BOGEY. What do you want?

HINZE. I'm a scholar traveling through and wanted to take the liberty of making Your Excellency's acquaintance.

BOGEY. Good, so make my acquaintance.

HINZE. You are a mighty prince, your love of justice is known throughout the entire world.

BOGEY. Yes, I can believe that. — But do sit down.

HINZE. Many wonderful things are told about Your Highness —

BOGEY. The people always want to have something to talk about, and those in power are the first to be discussed.

HINZE. But there's one thing I cannot believe, that you can transform yourself into an elephant and a tiger.

BOGEY. Then I'll give you an example of it right now. *(He transforms himself into a lion.)*

HINZE *(trembling, takes out a notebook)*. Permit me to make note of this phenomenon. — But now would you be good enough to assume your natural charming form again, because otherwise I'm going to die of fright.

BOGEY *(in his own form)*. How's that for a trick, my friend?

HINZE. Astonishing. But, one more thing: it's also said that you can transform yourself into very small animals; with your permission that's even more incomprehensible to me; can you just tell me, what happens then to your imposing body?

BOGEY. I'll do that too. *(He changes into a mouse; Hinze leaps after him on all fours; the Bogey flees into another room; Hinze goes after him.)*

HINZE *(returning)*. Liberty and equality! — The Law has been consumed! Now the *Tiers etat,*[6] Gottlieb, will surely assume the government.

(General stamping and hissing in the pit.)

SCHLOSSER. Well! so it's a revolutionary play? Then, for heaven's sake, nobody ought to stamp. *(The stamping continues; Wiesener and some others applaud; Hinze crawls into a corner and finally exits altogether. The Author is quarreling behind the scenes, and then steps forward.)*

AUTHOR. What am I to do? — the play is almost over — perhaps everything would have gone well — I had expected so much applause from precisely this moral scene. — If only it weren't so far from here — to the King's palace, — then I would get the Soother, — before at the conclusion of the second act he made all the fables about Orpheus believable. — But I'm such a fool. — I'm completely confused; — I'm standing on the stage, — and the Soother must be somewhere behind the sets. — I'll look for him, — I must find him, — he has to save me! — *(He exits, returns quickly.)* He's not there. — Soother! — A hollow echo mocks me. He has deserted me. — Ha! — there I see him, — he must come forward!

(The pauses are filled with stamping from the pit, and the author delivers this monologue recitatively so that a sort of musical effect is created.)

SOOTHER *(behind the scenes).* No, I'm not going out.

AUTHOR. But why not?

SOOTHER. I've already undressed.

AUTHOR. That doesn't matter. *(Pushes him forward forcefully.)*

SOOTHER *(comes forward in his street clothes with the glockenspiel.)* Well, you'll have to answer for it. *(He plays on the bells and sings:)*

> *Within these sacred halls*
> *   Revenge can find no place*
> *For, if a person falls,*
> *   Love shows him duty's face;*
> *Then guided by a friendly hand,*
> *   Joyful he wins the better land!*[7]

(The pit begins to applaud while the setting is changed onstage; the

*fire and the water from the **Magic Flute** begins to play; above is seen
the open temple of the sun; the heavens are opened and Jupiter is
sitting there; below is hell with Terkaleon, goblins and witches on
the stage; many lights, etc. The audience applauds excessively;
everything is in an uproar.)*

WIESENER. Now the cat has to go through fire and water and the play is
finished.

(The King, the Princess, Gottlieb, Hinze, Servants enter.)

HINZE. This is the palace of the Count of Carabas. — Now how in the devil
has this place changed so much?

KING. A beautiful palace.

HINZE. Since it's gone this far already, *(taking Gottlieb by the hand)* you
will have to go through the fire here, first of all, and then there
through the water.

*(Gottlieb to the sound of a flute and drum, walks through the fire and
water.)*

HINZE. You have stood the test, now, my prince, you are completely worthy
to rule.

GOTTLIEB. Ruling, Hinze, is a curious affair.

KING. Now receive the hand of my daughter.

PRINCESS. How happy I am!

GOTTLIEB. I too. — But my King, I would also like to reward my servant
now.

KING. To be sure; I hereby make him a member of the nobility. *(He hangs
a medal around the cat's neck.)* What is he actually called?

GOTTLIEB. Hinze; by birth he is only from a lowly family, but his services
elevate him.

LEANDER *(stepping forward quickly).*

I've ridden here to find my Royal Lord
And humbly his permission have implored
To pour out these poetic lines of praise,
Fit close for this most wonderful of plays.
I lose myself in this great theme I treat:
I celebrate the cat! The true elite
Of beasts who walk or stand upon four feet.
Cats once were gods for the Egyptian nation —
A cat was goddess Isis' near relation.
And, still on guard in kitchen, cellar, attic,
They're much more useful (here I'm quite emphatic)
In every house, than ancient gods or fairies;
And so let's set them up as modern Lares!

(Loud, general stamping; the curtain falls.)

EPILOGUE

KING *(stepping forward from behind the curtain).* Tomorrow we will have the honor of repeating today's performance.

FISCHER. What impudence! *(Everyone stamps.)*

KING *(becoming confused, goes away and then returns).* Tomorrow: — *The Sharper the Edge the Quicker the Nick!*[8]

ALL. Right! Right! — *(Applause, the King exits.)*

PEOPLE ARE SHOUTING: The last setting! The last setting!

BEHIND THE CURTAIN. It's true! They're calling for the set. *(The curtain goes up, the stage is empty, only the scenery is seen.)*

HANSWURST *(steps forward bowing).*

HANSWURST. Pardon me that I take the liberty of thanking you in the name of the set; it is only proper if the set is to be even half polite. It will attempt also in the future to deserve the applause of an enlightened audience; therefore there will certainly be no lack of lights or of necessary embellishments, for the approval of such an

assemblage will be so — so — so stimulating for it, — oh, you can
see, it is so moved to tears that it can say no more. —

*(He exits quickly and dries his eyes, a few people in the pit are crying,
the set is taken away, the bare walls of the stage are seen; people
begin to leave; the Prompter climbs out of his box;— the Author
appears on the stage, with a subdued air.)*

AUTHOR. If I may take the liberty —

FISCHER. You're still here?

MÜLLER. But you should have gone home.

AUTHOR. With your kind permission, just a few more words! My play has
failed —

FISCHER. You don't have to tell us.

MÜLLER. We noticed.

AUTHOR. Perhaps the fault is not entirely mine —

SCHLOSSER. Who else's then? Whose fault is it that I'm still half out of
my mind?

AUTHOR. I was trying to return all of you to the distant sensibilities of your
childhoods so that you might experience the fairy tale being presented
without regarding it as something more important than it was intended
to be.

LEUTNER. That's not so simple, my good man.

AUTHOR. To be sure you would have had to put aside your entire education
for two hours. —

FISCHER. But how is that possible?

AUTHOR. To forget your knowledge —

MÜLLER. And why not!

AUTHOR. Exactly as they've done in the journals.

MÜLLER. Just listen to what he's asking!

AUTHOR. In short, you would have had to become children again.

FISCHER. But we thank God that we no longer are.

LEUTNER. Our education cost us cold sweat and effort enough.

(There is stamping again.)

PROMPTER. Try making up a few verses, Author; maybe you'll get a little more respect from them then.

AUTHOR. Perhaps a Xenie will occur to me.

PROMPTER. What's that?

AUTHOR. A newly invented type of poetry which is better felt than described. *(To the pit)* Audience, if your judgment is to teach me even in some measure, indicate first that you understand me in some measure. *(Rotten pears and apples and rolled-up paper are thrown at him from the pit.)*

AUTHOR. The gentlemen down there are too much for me in this type of poetry; I withdraw.

The Final End

NOTES

[1]Terkaleon: villain in *The New Arcadians,* a play by Christian August Vulpius, produced in 1796.

[2] Leichdorn: = "Callus" or "Corn."

[3] Hanswurst: "Jackpudding," a stock comic character, popular in earlier plays, but sent "into exile" by neoclassical critics of the eighteenth century.

[4] These lines and the next several speeches of the King echo lines from Schiller's *Don Carlos* (1787) and *The Robbers* (1781), Shakespeare's *Hamlet,* etc.

[5] The rest of the scene is lifted from Mozart's *The Magic Flute* (1791).

[6] *Tiers etat:* In France the "third estate," or common people, assumed the government in the French Revolution. Also, in German *Tier* means "animal"; and of course Gottlieb is the third son.

[7] From *The Magic Flute.*

[8] A play by Iffland (1793).

ë

7

FRIEDRICH SCHLEGEL
(1772–1829)

Along with his brother August (1767–1845), Friedrich Schlegel was at the center of the "Early Romantic" group (Frühromantiker) and its principal theorist. His brief essays or "Fragments" published in the Schlegel brothers' journal, the *Athenaeum* (1798–1800), advocate new departures in literature and discuss many of the ideas central to Romanticism. His novel *Lucinde* (1799) was shockingly erotic for its day.

LYCEUM FRAGMENT

#37

In order to be able to write well about a subject, one must no longer be interested in it. An idea that requires thoughtful expansion must already be completely past and no longer really engaging. As long as the artist, in making up a story, is enthusiastic about his subject, he will find himself in difficulties, at least in trying to communicate it. For it is a mistaken tendency of young geniuses, and a real prejudice of old blunderers, to want to say everything. When he does so, the writer fails to see the value and the decorum of self-restraint, which after all, for artists as for people in general, is the Alpha and Omega, the most essential and the highest principle: it is the most essential principle, because whenever one fails to restrain himself, the world restrains, and thus enslaves him; and it is the highest principle because one can restrain oneself only in those aspects of life where one has unlimited power to begin with—self-creation and self-destruction. There is even something constraining about a friendly conversation that cannot be broken off on the whim of a moment. On the other hand a writer who can and will speak quite freely, who keeps nothing to himself and is inclined to tell all he knows, is much to be deplored. But one should beware of making three mistakes. First, whatever seems and ought to seem to be arbitrary caprice and consequently either unreasonable or beyond reason, must nevertheless turn out in the final analysis to be absolutely necessary and rational; otherwise, whim becomes obstinate, narrowmindedness arises, and out of self-restraint will come self-destruction. Second, one must not rush self-restraint too much, but first give originality, inventiveness, and enthusiasm time to develop. Third, one must not overdo self-restraint.

ATHENAEUM FRAGMENTS (1798)

#116

Romantic poetry is a progressive, universal poetry. Its role is not merely to reunite all of the separate poetic genres or to bring poetry into contact with philosophy and rhetoric. Its intent and indeed its duty is sometimes to mix, sometimes to fuse, poetry and prose, originality and criticism, and literary- and folk-poetry; to make poetry alive and sociable and to make life and society poetic; to poeticize wit, to fill and saturate the forms of art with solid cultural matter of every sort, then to enliven them with the vibrations of humor. Romantic poetry embraces everything that could be called poetic, from the greatest systems of art that contain several systems within themselves, to the sigh, the kiss, that the inspired child breathes out in artless song. It can so lose itself in the subject described that one might believe it is all one and the same to the artist to characterize poetic individuals of any type; and yet there is no form which could be made so apt for expressing completely the author's own spirit—so that many an artist, who intended to write just another novel, has in effect described himself. Only romantic poetry can, like the epic, become a mirror of the entire surrounding world, a picture of the age. And yet most of all it can also hover, on the wings of poetic reflection, between what is being described and the one describing, free of all real and ideal interests, again and again raising this reflection to higher powers and multiplying it as in an endless row of mirrors. It is capable of the highest and the most liberal education, not only from the inside out, but also from the outside in, since it is what a whole ought to be in its aggregate: it organizes the parts all in the same manner and thus opens for itself the prospect of an infinitely growing classicism. Romantic poetry is to the arts what wit is to philosophy and what society, acquaintances, friendship, and love are to life. Other styles of poetry are complete in their development and can now be perfectly analyzed. But the romantic style of poetry is still in the process of becoming; indeed, its essence is that it can never be perfected, but can only become eternally. It cannot be exhausted by any theory; and only a prophetic criticism might dare to try to characterize its ideal. It alone is infinite, just as it alone is free, recognizing as its foremost law that the license of the poet will tolerate no law above it. The romantic genre is the only one which is more than a genre and almost poetry itself: for in a certain sense, all poetry is or should be romantic.

#146

Just as the novel colors all of modern poetry, so does satire color all of Roman poetry, indeed the whole of the Roman literature, and virtually sets the keynote for it. Through all of its transformations among the Romans, satire always remained a classical, universal poetry, a social poetry, the central point of the civilized universe. In order to appreciate what is most urbane, most original, and most beautiful in the prose of a Cicero, a Caesar, or a Suetonius, one must already long have loved and understood Horace's satires. They are the eternal, primary sources of urbanity.

#216

The French Revolution, Fichte's *Wissenschaftslehre,* and Goethe's *Wilhelm Meister* represent the most important tendencies of the age. Whoever takes offense at this combination, whoever considers a revolution important only when it is loud and materialistic, has not yet raised himself to the high, vast viewpoint of human history. Our paltry cultural history for the most part resembles a collection of variant readings, with running commentary, to a lost classical text; yet even here, many a small book, little noticed by the noisy masses when it appeared, has played a greater role than anything they ever did.

#233

Religion, for the most part, only supplements or substitutes for education. Nothing is religious, in the strict sense of the word, that is not a product of freedom. Therefore, one could say, the freer one is, the more religious; and the more education one has, the less religion.

#238

There is a sort of poetry whose sole concern is the relationship between the ideal and the real, and which thus, by analogy with philosophical nomenclature, should be called transcendental poetry. It begins as satire, with an absolute distinction between the ideal and the real, hovers between them, as elegy, and ends as idyll, with an absolute identity of the two. But just as one would attach little importance to a transcendental philosophy if it were uncritical, if it did not describe process as well as product, if it did not itself embody the characteristics of transcendental thinking within the system of transcendental thought, so should this also be true of transcendental poetry, which among modern poets often combines transcendental materials and preliminary inquiries into a theory of poetic gifts with artistic contemplation and beautiful self-reflection. We find this combination in Pindar, in the lyric fragments and ancient elegies of the Greeks; but among modern writers, we find it only in Goethe. And in each of its manifestations, this poetry simultaneously reveals its own nature, being everywhere both poetry and poetry about poetry.

#305

To write ironically by design, and with an arbitrary appearance of self-destruction, is just as naive as to write ironically following one's instincts. Like naivete with its contradictions of theory and practice, the grotesque, too, plays with strange misplacements of form and matter. It loves the appearance of the accidental and the singular, and flirts, as it were, quite irresponsibly. Humor deals with questions of being and nonbeing, and its essential character is contemplative. Hence its affinity for the elegy and all that is transcendental; hence, too, however, its arrogance and propensity for the obfuscation of wit. Just as geniality is necessary for naivete, serious, pure beauty is necessary for humor. Humor loves most to hover over light

and clear flowing rhapsodies of philosophy or poetry, and it shuns
cumbersome lumps of prose and fragments torn out of context.

#372

The spirit of a different art often breathes in the works of the greatest poets.
Shouldn't this also be true of painters? In a certain sense, doesn't
Michelangelo paint like a sculptor; Raphael, like an architect; Correggio,
like a musician? And yet on this account they would certainly be considered
no less painters than Titian, who was pure painter.

#429

Just as the novella ought to be new and striking in every respect of
its existence and development, so too, perhaps, should the poetic fairy tale;
and the romance above all should be endlessly bizarre. For its purpose is not
only to engage the fancy, but also to enchant the spirit and charm the
feelings; and the essence of the bizarre seems precisely to consist of certain
arbitrary and strange entanglements and confusions in thinking, poetizing,
and acting. There is eccentricity in rapture which is compatible with the
highest education and freedom. It not only heightens the tragic but makes
it more beautiful and almost defies it—as in Goethe's *Braut von Korinth,* an
epoch-making work in the history of poetry. What is moving in it is
lacerating and yet seductively alluring. One could almost call several
passages burlesque, but it is precisely in these that the terrible appears
crushingly grand.

#433

The essence of poetic feeling lies perhaps in the fact that one can be
affected completely beyond oneself, that one can get worked up into an
emotional state over nothing, and that one can indulge in reveries without
cause. What is morally attractive is very easily compatible with a total lack
of poetic feeling.

#451

Universality is the reconciliation of all forms and all matter. It achieves harmony only by combining poetry and philosophy. When isolated in poetry or philosophy, even the most universal and most complete works seem to lack an ultimate synthesis; they stop, incomplete, just short of the goal of harmony. The life of the universal spirit is an unbroken chain of inner revolutions; all individuals—those who are original, that is, eternal—live in it. The universal spirit is truly polytheistic and bears all of Olympus within itself.

LONGING AND TRANQUILLITY

Julius' and Lucinde's Dialogue about Night (1799)

Lightly dressed, Lucinde and Julius stood at the pavilion window and refreshed themselves in the cool morning air, lost in the spectacle of the rising sun, which all the birds were greeting with merry song.

"Julius," asked Lucinde, "why, amidst such serene tranquillity, do I feel a profound longing?"

"It is only in longing that we find tranquillity," answered Julius. "Yes, tranquillity is simply what one feels whenever no other longing or seeking disturbs the spirit and one can find nothing higher than pure longing itself."

"Only in the tranquillity of night do longing and love sparkle as brightly and fully as this splendid sun," said Lucinde.

"And in the daytime," replied Julius, "the joy of love sheds only a faint light, just as the moon shines only feebly."

"Or it appears and disappears suddenly into total darkness," added Lucinde, "like that flash of lightning which lighted up our room, when the moon was covered."

"Only at night," said Julius, "does the little nightingale pour out its plaintive song and deep sighs. Only at night does the flower shyly open and freely breathe the loveliest fragrances, intoxicating mind and senses in the same bliss. Only at night, Lucinde, do love's ardor and bold speeches issue divinely from those lips which in the noisy daytime lock up their sweet shrine in delicate pride.

Lucinde: I am not the one, my Julius, whom you so sanctify although I may mourn like the nightingale and although I fervently feel that I am consecrated only to night. You are the one; it is the marvelous flower of your own fantasy, which, whenever life's tumult is muffled and nothing vulgar diverts your lofty mind, you then perceive in me, since I am always yours.

Julius: Stop flattering me and being so modest. Consider—you are the priestess of the night. In the rays of the sun itself, the dark gloss of your luxuriant curls, the luminous black of your solemn eyes, your stately figure, the majesty of your forehead and of all your noble limbs—all these proclaim it so.

Lucinde: My eyes sink as you praise me, because now the clear morning light blinds me and the merry song of the jolly birds troubles and frightens my soul. But in the dark, quiet coolness of the evening, my ear would certainly drink greedily of my dear friend's sweet words.

Julius: But it isn't frivolous babbling. My longing for you is endless and forever unequaled.

Lucinde: Whatever it may be—you are the point in which my being finds tranquillity.

Julius: I found sacred tranquillity, dear friend, only through that longing.

Lucinde: And I found that sacred longing in this beautiful tranquillity.

Julius: Oh, if only harsh light could lift the veil that so cloaks these flames, so that the play of the senses might soothe and cool my burning soul!

Lucinde: Someday that will happen. When youth flees and I renounce you, just as you once renounced the great love of one greater than you, then one eternally cold serious day will rend asunder life's warm night.

Julius: If only I might show you that unknown friend and show her the miracle of my wonderful good luck.

Lucinde: You still love her and will love her, and me as well, eternally. That is the great miracle of your wonderful heart.

Julius: Not any more wonderful than yours. I can see you lying against my breast, playing with the locks of your Guido, his dignified brow, adorned with garlands of eternal joy, uniting the two of us as brothers.

Lucinde: Do not drag forth into light whatever blossoms so sacredly in the heart's quiet depths; let it rest in night.

Julius: Where then may life's surging waves make sport of the wild one, whom tender feeling and fierce destiny forcibly carried forth into the harsh world?

Lucinde: The pure image of the sublime unknown sparkles, radiant and unique, in your pure soul's blue sky.

Julius: Oh, eternal longing!—But, finally, the fruitless longing and vain dazzling of daylight will sink and cease to exist, and a great night of love will feel eternally tranquil.

Lucinde: That's how I feel, if I may be what I am—feminine feelings in a warm, loving breast. My soul longs only for your longing, is tranquil wherever you find tranquillity.

＆

8

NOVALIS (FRIEDRICH VON HARDENBERG)
(1772–1801)

The most brilliant of the Schlegel circle of "Early Romantics," Novalis contributed fascinating aphorisms to the *Athenaeum* ("Pollen," 1798). His *Märchen* or "artificial folk tale" *Hyacinth and Rosebud* (written about 1798) contains the Romantic motifs of an animated nature and the quest for the ideal. In his novel *Heinrich von Ofterdingen* (1802) the object of the quest is symbolized by a blue flower—a famous Romantic image. Novalis' most famous work, *Hymns to the Night,* grew out of a mystical experience he had at the grave of his fiancée, Sophie von Kuhn. *Christendom, or Europe* presents his idealized view of medieval Christianity.

Hymns to the Night (1800)

1.

What person alive and endowed with all his senses does not love—more than all other wondrous appearances of the world about him—light itself, wellspring of joy for all, with its colors, rays, and waves, its soft pervasive presence in the waking day? The giant world of restless stars breathes light like the inmost soul of life, swimming and dancing in its blue ocean; the sparkling, ever-peaceful stone, the tender suckling plant, and the wild, fiery beast in its many varied forms—but most of all the noble stranger with the intelligent eyes, the lofty gait, and the gently closed, musical lips: all breathe light. Like a king of earthly nature, it summons each power to countless transformations, it binds and looses endless alliances, and hangs its heavenly image on every earthly being. Its presence alone reveals the miraculous splendor of the kingdoms of the world.

But I turn downward towards holy, ineffable, mysterious night. Far below lies the world, sunk in a deep pit, a lonely, desert place. Deep melancholy wafts through the heartstrings. I want to sink down with the dew and mingle with ashes. Vistas of memory, youthful wishes, childhood dreams—the brief joys and vain hopes of a whole long life—come clad in gray like evening mist. Light has pitched its happy tents in other realms: should it never return to its children who awaited it in innocent faith?

What suddenly wells up so prophetically in my heart and swallows up the soft breath of sadness? Do you also take pleasure in us, dark night? What do you hold under your mantle that strikes my soul with invisible power? Precious balm oozes from the bunch of poppies in your hand. You lift up the spirit's heavy wings. In some dark, inexpressible way we feel moved; happily surprised, I see a solemn countenance, that softly and devoutly bends toward me, and under an endless tangle of locks reveals the dear mother's youth. How poor and childish the light now seems to me—how cheering, how blessed the departure of day! Then was it only because the night drew away your servants, that you sowed the broad expanse with shining spheres—to proclaim in the times of your absences that you were all-powerful and would return? More heavenly than those glittering stars seem to us the infinite eyes that night opens up within us. They see further than the dimmest star of those countless hosts; needing no light, they look into the depths of a loving heart, which fills a higher realm with unutterable joy. Praise to the world's queen, high prophetess of holy worlds, guardian of blessed love. She sends you to me, my tender beloved, lovely sun of night. Now I awaken, for I am yours and my own; you have shown me that night is life, and you have made me human. Consume my body with spiritual fire, so that I may merge with you more intimately, like air, and the bridal night then last forever!

2.

Must morning always return? Does the power of this world never end? Our wretched activities destroy the approach of night's holy wings. Will love's secret sacrifice never burn without ceasing? Light had its appointed time, but night reigns beyond time and space. Sleep lasts eternally. Holy sleep! Amidst the daily labor of this earth, do not come too seldom with your blessings for the devotees of night. Only fools mistake you, and know of no sleep but the shadow which out of pity you toss us in that twilight of the true night. They do not feel you in the golden flood of the grapes, the magic oil of the almond, and the brown juice of the poppy. They do not see it is you who, hovering about the tender girl's bosom, makes the womb a heaven—do not suspect that you step out of old stories to open up the heavens, and bear the key to the dwelling places of the blessed, you silent messenger of infinite mysteries.

3.

Once, as I shed bitter tears, as my hope, dissolved in pain, flowed away, and I stood alone by a barren mound, which hid in a dark, narrow space the very form of my life, lonely as no one has ever been lonely before, stung by unspeakable anguish, sapped of all strength, a mere thought of misery—then as I looked about for help, able to move neither forward nor backward, and with infinite longing hung on to my snuffed-out life, slipping away; then out of blue distances, from the heights of my old blessedness, came a twilight tremor that in one stroke shattered the bonds of birth, the fetters of light. Away fled earthly splendor and with it my sorrow; grief flowed all together into a new, fathomless world: you, night-rapture, slumber of heaven, came over me; gently my surroundings grew more elevated, and over all soared my freed, newborn spirit. The mound turned to a cloud of dust; through the cloud I saw the transfigured countenance of my beloved. In her eyes rested Eternity—I grasped her hands, and the tears became a radiant, unbreakable bond. Millennia rolled down in the distance like storms. On her neck I wept rapturous tears for the new life. It was the first, the only dream, and since then for the first time I have felt an enduring, unchanging belief in heaven of night, and in its light, the beloved.

4.

Now I know when the last morning will be: when light no longer frightens away night and love, and when slumber is eternal and simply *one* long, inexhaustible dream. I feel a heavenly weariness in me. Long and exhausting was my pilgrimage to this holy grave, heavy the cross I bore. The crystal wave unheard by the common ear, springing from the dark womb of the mound whose foot turns back the earthly tide: whoever has tasted it, whoever has stood high on the world's great divide and looked over into the new land, into the dwelling place of night—truly, that person does not turn back to the activity of the world, to the land where light resides in eternal unrest.

Up there he builds himself shrines, shrines of peace; he longs and loves, and looks beyond, till the most welcome hour of all draws him down into the wells of the spring. What is earthly floats up, is carried back by storms; but what has become holy through the touch of love runs free through hidden ways to the realms beyond, where it mingles like fragrances with loved ones asleep. Still, cheerful light, you rouse the weary to labor, you channel joyful life into me—but you shall not lure me away from memory's mossy stone. I will gladly put my busy hands to work, look about wherever you need me, praise the full splendor of your glory, unweariedly pursue the beautiful coherence of your artful works, gladly study the ingenious movement of your mighty, shining clock, explore the balance of its forces and the laws of its wonderful mechanism's countless spaces and their periods; but my secret heart remains true to the night and her daughter, creative love. Can you show me a heart that is true forever? Does your sun have friendly eyes that recognize me? Do your stars clasp my eager hand? Do they return my tender touch and word? Was it you that adorned them with colors and delicate shapes, or was it *she* who gave your finery a higher, dearer meaning? What lust, what pleasure does your life offer that could outweigh the raptures of death? Does not everything that inspires us wear the color of night? She carries you as a mother, and you owe all your magnificence to her. Left to yourself, you would vanish, dissipate into infinite space, if she did not hold you, bind you, so that you might become warm and, flaming, beget the world. Truly, I was before you were: our mother sent me and my brothers and sisters to live in your world, to hallow it with love and so make it an eternally visible monument, to plant it with unfading flowers. They are not yet ripe, these holy thoughts; the traces of our revelation still are few. Some day your clock will point to the end of time, when you will become like one of us, full of longing and fervor, will burn out and die. I feel within me the end of your activity, heavenly freedom, blessed return. In wild pain I recognize your distance from our true home, your resistance against the old, magnificent Heaven. Your rage and frenzy are in vain. The cross stands, unconsumed, the victorious banner of our race.

> I'm a pilgrim
> to the beyond,
> and every torment
> shall become a sting
> of delight.
> Just a little longer,
> and I'll be free

and lie drunken
in the lap of love.
Eternal life surges
strongly in me;
I look from above down upon you.
At that hill of earth
your splendor dies;
a shadow brings
a cooling wreath.
Oh, draw me to you
with all your might,
my lover,
so I can sleep
and love!
I feel death's
rejuvenating flood
turning my blood
to ether and balm.
By day I live
in faith and courage,
and nightly I die
in holy fire.

5.

Over the far-flung races of men in ages past an iron fate ruled with
mute power. Dark and heavy bonds lay on men's fearful souls. Earth was
endless, the seat of the Gods, their homeland. Its mysterious fabric had
stood for eternities. Over the dawn-red mountains, in the holy bosom of the
sea, dwelt the sun, the all-kindling, living light. An ancient giant carried the
blessed world. Fast under mountains lay the first sons of Mother Earth,
powerless in their destructive rage against the magnificent new race of Gods
and their kindred, the happy human beings. The dark green depth of the sea

was the lap of a goddess, where in crystal grottoes voluptuous beings reveled. Streams, trees, flowers, and beasts had human feelings. Wine tasted sweeter, poured out in open, youthful abundance; a god was in the grapes; a loving, motherly goddess grew upwards in full golden sheaves; love's holy transport was a sweet service to the most beautiful divine lady. An endlessly brilliant feast of the children of heaven and the dwellers of earth, life rushed onward like a springtime through the centuries. All races like children adored the tender, thousandfold flame as supreme in the world. Only there was *one* thought, *one* horrid spectre,

That frightening to the merry tables strode
And wrapped the soul in wildest consternation.
To anxious breasts the gods themselves bestowed
No wise advice, no means of consolation.
This monster travelled a mysterious road—
Raged unappeased by gift or supplication:
For it was Death who stopped the revelry
With bitter tears and pain and misery.

Forever parted now from all we know
That sweetly stirs the heart with happiness,
Sundered from those they love—those here below
Whom fruitless longing, endless griefs oppress—
To feeble dreams the dead appeared to go,
Doomed to an endless strife in powerlessness.
This was the rock on which joy's billow burst—
The endless woe with which man's life was cursed.

Man's fiery spirit took a daring leap,
And thus the grisly spectre beautified:
A gentle youth put out the light to sleep—
The end was mild—as if a harp string sighed.
Memory dissolved in shadows cool and deep.
So, pressed by need, this was the song men tried.

And yet the riddle of eternal night
Remained: deep emblem of a distant might.

The old world drew to a close. The pleasure garden of the youthful
race faded; the people, becoming unchildlike as they grew, strove toward
more spacious, desolate regions. The gods with their retinues vanished.
Nature stood alone and lifeless; barren numbers and harsh measurements
bound her in iron chains. The immense blossoming of life disintegrated into
dark words as if into dust and air. Fled were consecrated faith and the all-
transforming, all-relating heavenly spirit, fantasy. A hostile north wind
blew over the benumbed fields, and the benumbed, wondrous homeland
flew off into the ether. The distant reaches of heaven were filled with
shining worlds. The soul of the world with its powers withdrew into a deeper
sanctuary, in the higher region of the mind, there to rule until the new
dawning of glory on earth. No longer was light the gods' abode and a
heavenly sign—they cast over themselves the veil of night. Night became
the mighty womb of revelations: the gods returned to it and went to sleep,
so that they might come forth in a new, more magnificent form throughout
the transformed world. Then, from among the most despised nation, grown
prematurely old, and become stubbornly estranged from the holy innocence
of youth, the new world showed its face, never beheld before: in the poetic
hut of poverty, a son of the first virgin mother, infinite fruit of mystical
embrace. The Orient's prophetic, full-blossoming wisdom first learned that
the new age had begun: a star showed it the way to the King's humble cradle.
In the name of the vast future they honored him with brightness and
fragrance, the highest wonders of nature. Solitary, the divine heart blossomed
into a chalice of almighty love, looking towards his Father's lofty
countenance, and resting in the chastened, blessed bosom of his dear, grave
mother. Fervently the prophetic eye of the blooming child gazed on future
days, and on his loved ones, the nearest branches of his divine race,
untroubled by the destiny of his earthly days. Soon the most childlike
spirits—seized by a wonderful deep love—gathered around him. Strange
new life sprang up like flowers wherever he happened to be. Inexhaustible
words and the most joyful tidings fell from his friendly lips like sparks of

a divine spirit. From a distant shore, born under the bright sky of Greece, a
singer came to Palestine and gave up his whole heart to the wonderful child:

> You are the youth who has for many a year
> Stood on our graves, buried in deepest thought,
> A sign of comfort, through the night of fear,
> That higher man's glad birth might yet be sought.
> Now in sweet longing we are drawn from here
> By that which had our deepest sorrow wrought.
> Only in death was true life to be found;
> You are that death, and first have made us sound.

The singer went on joyfully to India, drunk with sweet love, and
poured out his heart in ardent songs under that mild sky, so that a thousand
hearts bent toward him and the joyful message flourished thousand-branched.
Soon after the singer took his leave, that priceless life became a victim of
man's deep depravity: he died young, torn away from the world he loved,
from his weeping mother and his faint-hearted friends. His beloved mouth
drained the dark cup of unspeakable sorrows: the hour of the new world's
birth drew near in awful anguish. He wrestled hard with the old death's
terrors; the weight of the old world lay heavy upon him. He took one last
kind look at his mother—then the hand of eternal love came to set him free,
and he went to his rest. For just a few days a deep veil hung over the raging
sea and the trembling land; those who loved him shed countless tears. The
seal of mystery was broken! Heavenly spirits raised the stone of ages from
his dark grave. By the sleeper sat angels, the delicate creations of his
dreams. Then, awakened in new divine splendor, he assumed the summit of
the newborn world, buried the old corpse in the empty tomb with his own
hand, and with that almighty hand laid upon it the stone that no power can
raise.

Even yet your loved ones weep tears of joy, tears of feeling and
infinite thanks at your grave; with joy and fear they still see you rise, and
themselves with you; see you weeping with sweet fervor on your mother's
blessed breast—walking, serious, with your friends, speaking words that

seem plucked from the Tree of Life; see you hasten with utter longing into
the Father's arms, bringing on the new humanity and the inexhaustible cup
of the golden future. Your mother soon hastened to you in heavenly
triumph: she was the first to take a place beside you in the new homeland.
Since then many ages have run their course, and your new creation has
moved in ever higher splendor; and thousands have followed you out of
pains and torments, full of belief and longing and faithfulness—thousands
are pilgrims with you and the holy Virgin in the Kingdom of Love, serve in
the temple of heavenly death and are yours in eternity.

> The stone is raised,
> mankind has arisen,
> we are yours
> in perfect freedom
> The bitterest grief departs
> before your golden cup,
> when earth and life give way
> to the last supper's grace.
> Death holds a wedding feast,
> the lamps are burning bright,
> the virgins are prepared
> with ample oil for light.
> Would that the distance rang
> already with your coming,
> and that the stars all called to us
> with human voice and tongue!
> Mary, to you a thousand
> hearts are lifted up;
> sunk in this shadowy life,
> they longed for you alone.
> They hope for restoration
> with penitential joy,
> if only you would clasp
> them to your faithful breast.

So many have been burning,
consumed in bitter pain,
and, fleeing from this world,
have turned and sought your hand
always stretched out before us
in our torment and need;
and now we come to join them
in that eternal land.

Now no believer living
weeps by any grave
and from no one is stolen
the sweet treasure of love:
he's eased of his yearning,
inspired by the night
and the children of heaven
watch over his heart.

Consoled, our life advances
toward eternal life;
growing by inner fire
our souls are glorified.
The starry world will dissolve
to golden wine of life which we shall drink
And become stars of light.

No more separation—
for love has been set free.
Life surges full as an endless sea.
All is *one* eternal poem,
All *one* night of bliss,
and our universal sun
is God's countenance.

6.

LONGING FOR DEATH

Down, down into the womb of earth,
The rage and the shock of pain
Heralds our glad departure.
And quickly in our narrow boat
We make our way to heaven's shore.
Let us praise eternal night,
And praise eternal slumber!
We have been warmed by the day's heat
And parched by lasting sorrow.
Our lust for distant lands is gone
We long but for our Father's home.
What can we do in this world,
With all our love and honor?
The old has now been laid aside,
What has the new to offer?
Alone and crushed they stand who give
The past their ardent, pious love:
The past, in which the senses brightly
Burned in high flames,
The Father's hand and countenance
Was still known to men,
And many, pure in spirit, could still
Reflect their great Original;
The past, when ancient races shone,
Still in their blooming verdure
And children who were heaven-bound
Sought holy death and torture
And though delight and life spoke out,
Still aching love broke many a heart;

The past, when as a glowing youth
God made himself apparent
And gave himself to early death
With wondrous loving spirit,
Accepting grief and pain
That we might love him all the more.

We see those times in darkest night,
Shrouded with anxious longing;
These worldly years can never slake
Our thirsty spirit's burning.
Back to our homeland we must turn
To see that holy time again.

What holds us back from our return?
Loved ones have long been resting;
At their graveside our own life ends;
Now we grow sad and frightened.
No need to continue seeking,
Our hearts are full, the world is empty.

Mysteriously, incessantly
Through us streams a sweet shudder—
I sense that from the distance rings
An echo of our sorrow:
Perhaps our loved ones too are yearning,
And sent us back a sigh of longing.

Down, down to the sweetest bride,
To Jesus the beloved:
Take heart! Twilight begins to fall
On us who love and suffer.
A dream breaks free our bonds at last
And sinks us on the Father's breast.

THE STORY OF HYACINTH AND ROSEBUD

A long time ago, far away toward the sunset, there lived a very young man. He was very good, but also exceedingly strange. He was always sad about nothing, really nothing; he was quiet and withdrawn, and when others played and were happy, he would sit by himself musing about strange things. Caverns and forests were his favorite places, and then he would talk with animals and birds, with trees and cliffs—of course not in sensible words—just a lot of nonsense that would make you die laughing. But he remained sullen and serious regardless of the squirrel, the monkey, the parrot and the bullfinch, who all tried hard to amuse him and guide him in the right path. The goose told fairy tales, the brook chimed in with a ballade; a big fat rock skipped like a billy goat; the rose gently crept around behind him, slipping through his curls; and the ivy stroked his care-laden brow. But gloom and melancholy were stubborn. His parents were very troubled; they didn't know what to do for him. He was healthy and ate well, they had never hurt him, and until a few years ago he had been the happiest and liveliest person imaginable, first in all the games and liked by all the girls. He was beautiful: he looked like a picture and danced like a dream. Among the girls there was one, a delicate, lovely child, fragile like a wax doll, with hair like golden silk, cherry lips, and her eyes burnt raven black. Everyone who saw her became lost in her beauty. In those days Rosebud (for that was her name) loved her beautiful Hyacinth tenderly, and Hyacinth (which was his name) would have gladly died for her. The other children didn't know. A violet first let out the secret, the kittens had noticed of course, for the houses of their parents were built close to one another. At night when Hyacinth stood at his window and Rosebud stood at hers, the kittens, coming by on their way to hunt mice, would see the two of them stand there, and then they'd laugh and giggle so loud that the two heard it and got angry. The violet had told the strawberry in strictest confidence and she told her friend the raspberry, who couldn't stop razzing Hyacinth whenever he came by; so that's how everyone in the garden and the forest found out about it, and now every time Hyacinth went out he could hear "Rosebud is my sweetheart!" coming from everywhere. He would become angry but then again he'd have to laugh heartily when the little lizard would slither on a warm stone, curl his tail and sing:

> The sweetest girl that you could find,
> Rosebud suddenly went blind—
> Thinks mother is in Hyacinth's place,
> And quickly gives him an embrace;
> But when she feels the stranger's face,
> Imagine that! She's quite resigned
> And as if nothing were amiss
> Goes right ahead and gives a kiss.

Alas, how soon all this joy was gone. There came a man from a foreign land who had traveled far and wide; his beard was long, his eyes deep set with fearsome eyebrows, and he wore strange clothes with many folds and figures woven into them. He sat down in front of the house that belonged to Hyacinth's parents. Hyacinth was very curious, of course; he sat down by him and brought him bread and wine. Then the old man parted his white beard and told stories deep into the night. Hyacinth sat spellbound, and didn't tire of listening. As far as anyone could find out afterwards, he told of foreign countries and unknown regions; he told of amazing, wondrous things, stayed three days and crawled down into deep caverns with Hyacinth. Rosebud often wished the old sorcerer had never come, because Hyacinth was mad about his talk and tales; he cared for nothing else, barely even finding time to eat. Finally the old man went on his way and left a book for Hyacinth which no man could read. Hyacinth gave him fruit and bread and wine for the trip and accompanied him a long way. And when he came back he was pensive and began a new way of life. Rosebud grieved woefully, because from that time on he cared little for her and kept to himself. And then one fine day he came home as if reborn. He fell into his parents' arms and cried. "I must travel into foreign lands," he said. "The strange old woman in the woods told me how to get well, and threw the book into the fire and drove me to come to you and ask your blessing. Maybe I'll come

back soon and maybe never again. Give my love to Rosebud. I would have
liked to tell her good-bye, I don't know what's wrong with me, something's
driving me to go; whenever I want to think back to the old times, other, more
powerful thoughts come into my mind, my peace is gone, my heart and my
love, and I must go find them. I would gladly tell you where, but I don't
know myself, wherever the mother of all things lives, the veiled maiden. My
soul burns for her. Farewell." He tore himself away and left. His parents
wept and lamented, Rosebud stayed in her room and cried bitterly.

Hyacinth made his way as he could through valleys and wilderness,
over mountains and rivers toward that mysterious country. He asked about
Isis, the divine goddess, everywhere—people and animals, cliffs and trees.
Some laughed, some were silent, no one could give him directions. In the
beginning he came through rough wild country, clouds and mists threw
themselves into his path, brewing storms; then he found unending sand
deserts, glowing dust; and as he wandered, his mood changed too, time
seemed to drag, his inner turmoil lessened, his feelings softened and the
driving force in him became a gentle but insistent yearning that suffused his
heart and soul. His trials lay behind him like many years. Now the countryside
became richer and more various, the air bluer, the path more even, green
bushes tempted him with lovely shade; he did not understand their language
nor did they seem to speak, and yet they filled his heart with green colors
and cool serenity. That sweet longing grew ever stronger in him, leaves
became ever more lush and luxuriant, birds and animals ever louder and
lustier, fruit more fragrant, the sky deeper, the air warmer and his love more
intense, time flew as if the goal were in sight. And then one day he met a
crystal spring and a crowd of flowers coming into a valley between sheer
black cliffs that reached the sky. They greeted him with friendly and
familiar words. "Dear countrymen," he said, "where can I find the hallowed
dwelling place of Isis? It must be close by somewhere, and perhaps you
know this region better than I." "We are also only passing through ourselves,"
said the flowers. "A spirit family is traveling this way and we are going
ahead of them to prepare their path and lodging; but we did come through
a region just now where we heard her name mentioned. Just go up where we
came from, you'll hear more there." The flowers and the spring swirled as

they said this and they gave him fresh water to drink and went on their way. Hyacinth followed their advice, and kept asking and asking and finally he came to the house he had been looking for so long, hidden under palms and other marvellous plants. His heart beat with infinite longing and a sweet anxiety came over him in this place of eternal seasons. He fell asleep in heavenly fragrance, for only a dream could lead him into the holy of holies. Wondrously the dream led him through endless rooms of strange things to lovely sounds in changing harmonies. Everything seemed so familiar and yet in splendor never seen before, and then the last earthly hue vanished as if consumed into the air and he stood before the heavenly maiden. Then he lifted the light shimmering veil and Rosebud sank into his arms. Distant music floated around the mystery of their loving reunion, the opened floodgate of longing, and kept all outside things away from this enchanted spot. And Hyacinth and Rosebud lived together for a long time among his friends and parents, who were overjoyed; and countless grandchildren thanked the strange old woman for her advice and her fire; for in those days people had as many children as they wanted.

CHRISTENDOM OR EUROPE
(written 1799; pub. 1802)

Those were lovely, splendid times, when Europe was a Christian land, when *one* Christendom dwelt in this continent shaped by mankind, and *one* great common interest united the most distant provinces of this vast spiritual kingdom. *One* leader, without great worldly possessions, guided and unified the great political powers. Immediately under him stood a numerous guild, open to all, that carried out his orders and zealously strove to consolidate his benevolent power. Each member of this society was respected everywhere; and if the common people sought his comfort or help, his protection or advice, and in return freely and bountifully supplied his many needs, so likewise the more powerful honored, protected, and listened to him; and everyone took care of these chosen men, so wonderfully endowed, as if they were children of Heaven, whose presence and sympathy spread manifold blessings. Childlike faith bound people to their teachings. How cheerfully could every man approach the end of his earthly tasks, when, through these holy men, a sure future was prepared for him; through them, every mistake forgiven; through them, every blemish of life wiped clear and clean! They were the trusty pilots on the great unknown sea, in whose care one could scorn all storms and look confidently to a safe approach and landing in the world that is our true homeland.

The wildest, most voracious impulses shrank in awe and submission before their word. Peace flowed from them. They preached nothing but love for the holy, wonderfully beautiful Lady of Christendom, who with her divine strength was ready to rescue any believer from the most terrible dangers. They told of holy people long dead, who, through faith and constancy to that blessed Mother and her divine, loving Child, withstood the temptations of this earthly life and won glory in Heaven, and now had become powerful and benevolent protectors of their earthly brothers— willing helpers in time of need, intercessors for human frailties, and effective advocates of mankind before the heavenly throne. How happy people used to be, emerging from beautiful services in the dim churches adorned with inspiring works of art, filled with sweet odors, and enlivened with holy, elevating music. Here the consecrated refrains of God-fearing people who lived in earlier times were gratefully preserved in precious shrines, which showed, through splendid wonders and signs, the goodness and power of God, and the mighty beneficence of these happy saints. Just as loving souls will preserve locks of hair or handwriting of their beloved dead to sustain the sweet flame until death reunites them, so, whenever they could, people used to collect with fervent care everything that had belonged to these beloved souls, and a person considered himself lucky to possess, or even touch, such a comforting relic. Every now and then it seemed that heavenly grace would descend particularly upon some unusual picture or grave; to such places people streamed from every region bearing beautiful gifts, and in return gathered heavenly gifts: peace of soul and health of body. This powerful band of peace-making men sought eagerly to make all people share their beautiful faith, and sent representatives to all parts of the world to preach and to make the Kingdom of Heaven the only kingdom on this earth.

Quite properly, the wise head of the church opposed bold secular developments that threatened sacred thought, and dangerous discoveries in the sphere of learning that the times were not ready for. Thus he kept daring thinkers from maintaining publicly that the earth is an insignificant planet, because he knew very well that such a belief would lead people to lose respect not only for their earthly dwelling and homeland, but also for their heavenly home and for the human race, so that they would prefer circumscribed knowledge to infinite belief, and would become used to scorning all great things worthy of wonder, considering them mere dead doctrinal formulations. At his court could be found all the august and brilliant men of Europe. All treasures flowed to him: fallen Jerusalem came into its own—Rome itself was Jerusalem, become the holy seat of God's kingdom on Earth. Princes willingly laid their disputes before the Father of Christendom, their crowns and splendor at his feet; indeed they considered it an honor to live out the evening of their lives as members of that lofty brotherhood, devoted to godly contemplation in the solitude of cloister walls. Just how beneficial this regime was, how appropriate this institution was, to man's inner nature, could be seen by the mighty flowing of the whole range of human powers, the harmonious development of all talents, the extraordinary heights that individual men attained in all the sciences and arts, and the vast commerce, both spiritual and material, that flourished throughout Europe and even to the farthest Indies.

Such were the beautiful qualities of those truly Catholic—or rather, truly Christian—times. Yet mankind was not ready, not sufficiently developed, for this happy state. It was a first love, which, for a great part of the European population, faded in the press of commerce, pushed from man's thoughts by selfish cares, and stripped forever of its attractions—afterward decried as imposture and delusion, condemned in the light of later experience. This great internal division, with the destructive wars that accompanied it, was a striking instance of the damage culture can cause to the spiritual sense, or at least the temporary damage culture can cause at a certain stage. While that immortal sense can never be destroyed, it can be troubled, lamed, crowded out by other senses. A society that remains stable over a long period of time weakens peoples' affections, their belief in their own kind, and accustoms them to turn all their attention and effort exclusively to the attainment of amenities; the arts and means of enjoyment proliferate, and it takes so much time to become familiar with them and expert in them, that the acquisitive person has no time left for quiet composure of his spirit, and careful attention to the inner world. Whenever there is a conflict, immediate interest seems to lie nearer to him, and so the beautiful blossoms of his youth—faith and love—fall and make way for the cruder fruits—facts and possessions. In late autumn, one looks back on springtime as a childish dream, and hopes with naive simplicity that the full granary will last forever. A certain solitude seems necessary for the development of the higher sense, and so too much society will smother many a tender growth of holiness, and frighten away the gods who flee the hurly-burly of social distractions and the transaction of petty affairs. Besides, we are concerned with times and periods, and do these not imply an oscillation, an alternation of opposing tendencies? Do they not imply by their very nature a limited duration, an increase and a decline? But is not a resurrection, a rejuvenation, in a newer, more powerful form, also certainly to be expected of them?

Progressive, ever increasing evolution is the stuff of history. Whatever fails to attain perfection now, will attain it in a future attempt or a repeated one. Whatever is once a part of history never disappears: it is renewed in ever richer forms through countless transformations. Christianity, having once appeared in full power and glory, survived as a ruin, a dead letter, in ever-increasing weakness and derision, until a new inspiration should once again animate the world. Infinite inertia lay heavy on the guild of the clergy, long accustomed to security. They stagnated in their comfort and the sense of their own importance, while the laity wrested experience and learning from their hands and made great strides in cultural development. Neglecting their true duty—to be first among men in intellect, insight, and culture—they succumbed to low desires, and the meanness and baseness of their way of thinking was the more repugnant because of their dress and vocation. Thus respect and confidence, the cornerstones of this and of every state, gradually crumbled, and, long before the actual Revolution, this guild was ruined and the real power of Rome had silently come to an end. Merely clever (and hence also merely temporary) expedients still held the corpse of the organization together and kept it from too rapid dissolution—a prime example being the abolition of marriage for the clergy, an expedient which, applied analogously to a similar group, the military, would give it a terrific solidarity and notably extend its life. What was more natural than that, sooner or later, an inflammatory mind should preach open rebellion against the despotic dead letter of the moribund organization, and with all the more success because he himself was a member of the guild.

The insurgents called themselves Protestants, for they were solemnly protesting against the usurpation of authority over the conscience by a troublesome and apparently unlawful power. For the time being they took back again, as if it were free, the right they had tacitly given up to examine, determine, and choose their own religion. They also established a number of sound principles, brought about a number of praiseworthy innovations, and did away with a number of bad laws; but they forgot the inevitable consequence of their procedures: they separated the inseparable, divided the indivisible Church, and wantonly tore themselves from the universal Christian community, through which and in which alone true, lasting rebirth was possible. The condition of religious anarchy must be only temporary, because there remains valid and operative a basic need to dedicate a number of people exclusively to this high vocation and to make these people, with respect to its concerns, independent of secular power. The establishment of tribunals and the retention of a kind of clergy did not fulfill this need and was not a satisfactory substitute. Unfortunately the secular princes became involved in this schism, and many used these disputes to strengthen and extend their own territorial power and revenues. They were happy to be relieved of those high external influences, and took the new tribunals under their sovereign protection and guidance. They were zealously concerned with preventing the complete unification of the Protestant churches, and so religion was irreligiously contained within political boundaries; this was where the gradual erosion of religion's international interests had its start. Thus religion lost its great political influence as a power for peace, and its special role as unifying, individualizing principle—as Christendom. Religious peace was settled according to quite erroneous and antireligious principles, and through the continuation of so-called Protestantism something thoroughly contradictory saw the light: a permanent revolutionary regime.

But Protestantism is by no means based exclusively on that one idea; on the contrary, Luther dealt with Christianity rather arbitrarily, mistook its true spirit, and introduced another *letter* and another religion, namely the holy universal validity of the Bible, and in so doing mixed into religious matters another, highly alien secular science—Philology—the debilitating influence of which becomes unmistakable from that time on. A large proportion of Protestants, out of some obscure feeling about this error, elevated him to the rank of an Evangelist and canonized his translation.

This choice was in the highest degree destructive to the religious sense, since nothing deadens its sensitivity so much as the letter. In the past, the situation was such that the letter could never become so pernicious, on account of the pervasiveness, the flexibility, and the rich content of the Catholic faith, as well as the esoteric nature attributed to the Bible, and the sacred power of the councils and the holy pontiff. But now these antidotes were denied and the total popular accessibility of the Bible asserted; and the meager contents, the crude, abstract outline of religion in these books, became all the more markedly oppressive, and made infinitely more difficult the free animation, penetration, and revelation of the Holy Spirit.

Hence the history of Protestantism no longer presents us with splendid manifestations of the supernatural; only its outset glowed with a momentary heavenly fire, and soon afterward it is evident that the religious spirit dried up. The things of this world gained the upper hand; the artistic spirit suffered in sympathy; only occasionally does a real, eternal living spark spring up and a small community of followers assimilate into one body. The spark goes out, and the community drifts apart again and is carried away with the stream. Such were Zinzendorf, Jacob Böhme, and others. The moderates are in the ascendant, and the times are approaching a total deadness of the higher organs, a period of practical unbelief. The Reformation brought Christendom to an end. From then on it did not exist any more. Catholic and Protestant or Reformed stood further from one another in sectarian division than from Mohamedans and heathens. The remaining Catholic states continued to vegetate, not immune to the subtly pernicious influence of the neighboring Protestant states. Modern politics first emerged at this time, and powerful individual states sought to occupy the vacant chair of universal authority, which had been transformed into a throne.

* * * * * * * *

The Reformation was a sign of its times. It had significance for all of Europe, even though it actually broke out openly only in Germany, where real freedom could be found. The good minds of all the nations had secretly matured, and, in the delusory feeling of their vocation, they inclined all the more boldly against outdated authority. By instinct the intellectual is enemy of the traditional clergy; the two must wage war to the death if they are separate parties, for they are fighting for a single position. This separation became increasingly pronounced, and the intellectuals won all the more ground, as the history of the European people approached the triumph of learning, and knowledge and faith came into decisive opposition to one another. People regarded faith as the origin of the general impasse, and they hoped to remedy it by penetrating knowledge. Everywhere the spirit of religion suffered from the manifold persecutions that had characterized its own actions up until then—that were its personality at that time. The result of the modern way of thinking was called philosophy, which included everything that opposed the old ways, hence in particular every attack on religion. What had begun as a specific hatred of Catholicism gradually turned into hatred of the Bible, of Christianity, and finally of religion itself. Nay, hatred of religion extended quite naturally and inevitably to all objects of enthusiasm; it decried imagination and feeling, morality and art, the future and the past, all as heresies; it grudgingly set man at the top of the hierarchy of nature, and turned the infinite creative music of the cosmos into a monotonous rattling of some monstrous mill, driven by the stream of chance, on which it also floated, an autonomous mill-in-itself, without builder or miller—indeed, a true perpetual motion machine, a self-grinding mill.

One enthusiasm was generously left to the poor human race, and was made the indispensable touchstone of highest culture for everyone concerned: the enthusiasm for this grand, splendid philosophy, and more particularly for its priests and mystagogues. France was so fortunate as to become the womb and seat of this new faith, stuck together out of pure knowledge. However much poetry was decried in this new church, there were still a few poets around who for effect still used the old ornaments and old flashes of illumination, though in doing so they were in danger of kindling the new world system with the old fire. But cleverer members knew how to pour cold water right away on listeners who had grown warm. The members busied themselves tirelessly with cleaning the poetry from nature, earth, the human soul, and the sciences—wiping out every trace of holiness, spoiling with sarcasm the memory of every elevating event and person, and stripping the earth of all its bright ornaments. Light, because of its mathematical tractability and its impudence, became their special favorite: pleased rather by its properties of refraction than by its play of colors, they took its name for their great movement, the Enlightenment. In Germany the movement was carried out even more thoroughly: education was reformed, and there was an attempt to give the old religion a more up-to-date, rational, relevant spirit by carefully scrubbing it free of everything miraculous and mysterious;

all scholarship was bent to cut off an escape into the past, as people tried to ennoble history into a domestic and civic portrait of manners and families. God was made into an idle spectator of the great, moving spectacle produced by the scholars, and at the end He was supposed richly to entertain and admire the playwrights and actors. The common folk by actual preference were enlightened and educated in that cultured enthusiasm, and so there appeared a new European guild: that of philanthropists and enlighteners. Too bad that nature remained so wonderful and elusive, so poetic and infinite, despite all efforts to modernize her! If anywhere an old superstition about a higher world and such turned up, then immediately on all sides the alarm was sounded and whenever possible the dangerous spark was reduced to ashes by philosophy and wit; nevertheless *tolerance* was the watchword of the educated, and, especially in France, was synonymous with *philosophy*. This history of modern atheism is highly interesting, and the key to all the monstrous occurrences of modern times. It first began in this century, especially in the latter half, and in a short time has grown to an immense size and diversity; a second Reformation, more comprehensive and appropriate to this situation, was inevitable, and it had to strike first in the country that was most modernized and for want of freedom had lain longest in an asthenic state. The supernatural fire would have long since broken free and thwarted the clever plans of the Enlightenment, had not the latter made use of worldly pressures and influence. But the moment a difference arose between the learned and the rulers—the enemies of religion and all their allies—religion had to step forward again as a third, harmonizing, mediating member—an emergence which every friend of religion now ought to acknowledge and proclaim, if it is not already sufficiently apparent. No person with a mind for history can doubt that the time has come for the resurrection of religion, and that exactly those circumstances which seemed to be against its animation and to threaten the final accomplishment of its demise, have become the most favorable signs of its regeneration. Real anarchy is the element from which religion is born. Out of the annihilation of everything positive it lifts its glorious head as the new founder of the world. Humanity, unbound, rises toward heaven as if spontaneously, and like the original seed of earthly formation, the higher organs move by themselves for the first time out of the undifferentiated mass which holds in solution all human abilities and powers. The Holy Spirit hovers over the waters, and a heavenly island, dwelling place of the new race of men—vale of eternal life—appears for the first time above the receding waves.

Let the true observer consider calmly and objectively the new revolutionary times. Does not the revolutionary seem to him like Sisyphus? He no sooner reaches the point of equilibrium than the mighty weight rolls down again on the other side. It will never stay up there unless an attraction toward heaven holds it balanced at the top. All your props are too weak, as long as your state keeps its penchant for the earth; but join it by a higher attraction to the heights of heaven, give it a connection with total reality, and then it will spring up for you with unflagging resiliency, and will richly repay all your efforts. I suggest you turn to history: search its instructive fabric for similar periods, and learn to use the magic wand of analogy.

Shall the Revolution remain French, as the Reformation was Lutheran? Shall Protestantism become fixed once more as that freak of nature, a revolutionary establishment? Shall letter replace letter? Do you also seek in the old order, in the old spirit, the germ of its destruction, and imagine you have the key to a better order, a better spirit? Oh, that you were filled with the spirit of spirits and would desist from this foolish effort to recast history and mankind in your own mold! Are they not independent, self-directed, as well as infinitely lovable and prophetic? To study it, to follow it, to learn from it, to keep in step with it, to follow, believing, its promises and signs— these are things that no one thinks of.

In France much was done for religion when it was deprived of its official status and left only the rights of a private householder—to be sure, not like any single person, but in all its countless individual forms. Like a strange, homely orphan it must first reconquer people's hearts and win universal love, before it can be publicly worshipped again and become involved in worldly matters as a source of friendly counsel and mental harmony. Of continuing historical significance is the effort of that great iron mask which, under the name of Robespierre, sought the center and power of the republic in religion; also the coldness with which theophilanthropy, this mysticism of the new Enlightenment, has been accepted; also the new conquests of the Jesuits; also the closer connections with the Orient that have developed with the new political conditions.

Of the other European countries besides Germany, all one can predict is that, with *peace*, a new, higher religious life will begin to pulse within them and will soon swallow up all other worldly interests. In Germany, on the other hand, one can already demonstrate with full certainty evidences of a new world. Germany goes along slowly but surely in advance of the other European countries. While these latter busy themselves with war, speculation, and partisan spirit, the Germans are educating themselves as quickly as possible to be participants in a higher epoch of culture, and in the course of time this progress must give them a great advantage over the others. A great ferment in the arts and sciences is evident. Infinite mental resources are opening up. New, fresh lodes are being tapped. Never has learning been in better hands, or at least aroused greater expectations; the different aspects of things are being traced out, and nothing is left unsifted, unjudged, unanalyzed. Work is going ahead everywhere; writers are becoming more individual and more powerful; every old monument of history, every art, every science is finding advocates, and will be embraced with new love and made fruitful. An unparalleled versatility, a wonderful profundity, a brilliant polish, many-faceted knowledge, and a rich, powerful imagination may be found hither and yon, often in bold combination. Everywhere there seems to be astir a mighty intimation of the inner man's creative will, his boundlessness, his infinite variety, his holy individuality, and his unlimited capability. Waked from the morning dream of helpless childhood, a portion of the race uses its first strength on the serpents that coil about its cradle and try to immobilize its limbs. All these things are still merely indications, disconnected and crude; but they reveal, to the eye attuned to history, a universal individuality, a new history, a new humanity, the sweetest embrace of a loving God and a young church surprised, and the immediate, passionate conception of a new Messiah within its thousand members. Who does not, with sweet shame, feel happily expectant? The newborn will be the image of its father—a new Golden Age with dark eyes of infinite depth, a prophetic age, wonderworking, miraculously healing, comforting and kindling eternal life—a great age of reconciliation, a Savior who, like a true presiding spirit at home among men, will be believed in, not seen, though visible to the faithful in countless forms, consumed as bread and wine, embraced as a lover, breathed as air, heard as word and song, and received with heavenly delight, with the intensest pain of love, into the inmost depths of the expiring body as death.

Now we stand high enough to cast a friendly smile back on those ages just mentioned, and also to recognize in those incredible follies some remarkable crystalizations of historical material. We will thankfully shake the hands of those scholars and philosophers; for the good of posterity, such errors had to be exhausted and the truly scientific view of things to be validated. Poetry stands brighter and more appealing, like a bejeweled India, as contrasted with the cold, dead Spitsbergen of that closet philosophy. In order that India may lie so warm and splendid in the middle of the globe, a cold, frozen sea, dead cliffs, long night, and fog instead of starry heavens must make the two ends of the earth inhospitable. The deep meaning of mechanics obsessed those anchorites in the desert of reason; the charm of the first insight overwhelmed them, and the past took revenge on them: they sacrificed, in amazing denial, what was holiest and most beautiful in the world to this first self-consciousness, and were the first again by deed to acknowledge and to proclaim the holiness of nature, the infinitude of art, the inevitability of knowledge, the worthiness of this world, and the omnipresence of the truly historical; and in so doing they put an end to a higher, more pervasive, and more dreadful reign of phantoms than they themselves were aware of.

It is first of all through a more exact knowledge of religion that one can best judge that dreadful progeny of religion's sleep, those dreams and deliriums of the faculty of holiness—only then can one learn to appreciate properly the momentousness of that gift. Where no gods are, phantoms rule; and the particular period when European ghosts developed (which rather completely explains the forms they took) is the period of transition from Greek mythology to Christianity. So come too, you philanthropists and Encyclopedists, into the lodge of peacemakers, and receive the kiss of brotherhood; cast off those gray toils and look with young love at the wondrous splendor of nature, of history, and of humankind!

* * * * * * * *

Now let us turn to the political spectacle of our time. The old and the
new worlds are locked in battle, the defects and bankruptcy of existing
political regimes have become apparent in the terrible events. What if here,
as in the sciences, closer and more thoroughgoing connections and contacts
among European states were the coming historical goal of war?—if a
hitherto slumbering Europe were to bestir itself, if Europe were to awaken
again, if a state of states, a political science of knowledge were to confront
us! Could it be that hierarchy, that symmetrical basic structure of states, is
the principle of federation among states—the intellectual representation of
the political "I"? It is impossible for worldly powers to put themselves in
equilibrium: only a third element, at the same time partaking of this world
yet transcending it, can resolve the situation. Among the conflicting powers
no peace can be concluded; any apparent peace is merely a truce—from the
points of view of both political counsels and common opinion, no unification
is conceivable. Both parties have great, necessary claims and must assert
them, driven by the spirits of this world and of humanity. Both are
indestructible powers in man's heart: on the one hand, devotion to the past,
attachment to historical continuity, love for the monuments of ancestors and
the ancient and glorious national family, and the satisfaction of obedience;
on the other hand, the delightful feeling of freedom, the limitless expectation
of mighty spheres of activity, pleasure in whatever is new and young, easy
intercourse with all fellow citizens, pride in the universal worth of mankind,
joy in private rights and in the possessions of the whole, and the powerful
sense of citizenship. Let neither wish to destroy the other; all conquests
mean nothing here, for the innermost capital of every kingdom does not lie
behind earthworks and cannot be taken by storm.

Who knows whether we have had enough war? But it will never stop
until we grasp the palm branch which only a spiritual power can offer. Blood
will stream over Europe until the nations realize their dreadful madness that
drives them around in circles, and, struck and softened by sacred music,
they approach in all their bright-hued variety the altars of bygone days,
there to take up works of peace and, with hot tears upon the smoking

battlefield, to celebrate a great love feast, a festival of peace. Only religion can awaken Europe again and give the people security and reinaugurate Christendom in its old role of peacemaker with new magnificence before the eyes of the whole world.

Do nations have all the human qualities—except a heart, man's holy faculty? Will nations not, like men, become friends over the coffins of their loved ones, and forget all their enmity when divine sympathy speaks to them both—and *one* misfortune, *one* grief, *one* feeling fills their eyes with tears? Will not the power of sacrifice and surrender seize them irresistibly, and will they not long to be friends and allies?

Where is that old, beloved belief in the reign of God on earth, in which alone blessedness can be found? Where is that heavenly trust between men, that sweet devotion in the effusions of a divinely inspired spirit, that all-embracing spirit of Christendom?

Christianity has three aspects. One is the creative religious element, the joy of all religion. One, mediation in a broad sense—belief in the efficacy of all things of the earth to be the wine and bread of eternal life. And one, the belief in Christ, his mother, and the saints. Choose which you please. Choose all three, it is all the same—in doing so you become Christians and members of a single, eternal, inexpressibly blessed community.

Applied, living Christianity was the old Catholic faith, the last of these aspects. Its presence everywhere in life, its love of art, its deep humanity, the indissolubility of its marriages, its benevolent sociability, its joy in poverty, obedience, and loyalty—all characterize it unmistakably as true religion, and constitute the basic qualities of which it is composed.

It has been purified in the stream of time; in deep, inseparable union with the two other forms of Christianity it will bring felicity to this earth forever.

Its accidental form is for all practical purposes destroyed; the old papacy lies buried and Rome has become a ruin for the second time. Shall not Protestantism finally come to an end and make way for a new, more lasting church?

The other parts of the world await Europe's reconciliation and resurrection, that they may join it and become fellow citizens of the Kingdom of Heaven. Shall we not soon again have a host of truly heavenly spirits in Europe, shall not all who are truly joined in religion long to see heaven on earth, and eagerly raise their voices together in holy song?

Christendom must again become living and effective, and must again create, without considering national boundaries, a visible church, which will take to its bosom the soul thirsty for spiritual life, and which will be a joyful mediator between the old and the new world.

It must again pour out the old cornucopia of blessing over the people. From the holy womb of a venerable European council, Christianity will arise and the course of religious awakening will be carried out according to an all-embracing divine plan. Then no one will protest any more about Christian and secular constraints, for the essence of the church will be true freedom, and all necessary reforms will be carried out under its own guidance as peaceful and orderly civil procedures.

When, oh when? It is not for us to ask. Patience! It will, it must come—the holy time of eternal peace, when the New Jerusalem will be the capital of the world; and until then, be serene and brave amid the dangers of the time, companions of my faith; proclaim with word and deed the divine gospel and remain steadfast in the true, infinite faith, until death.

9

FRIEDRICH HÖLDERLIN
(1770–1843)

Inspired by the beauties of classical Greece, Hölderlin hoped for the return of a new Golden Age; but he also felt a foreboding of doom; he suffered attacks of mental illness in 1802 and remained hopelessly insane until his death. His poetry is of such depth that it has scarcely been appreciated until recent years.

AN DIE PARZEN

Nur einen Sommer gönnt, ihr Gewaltigen!
Und einen Herbst, zu reifem Gesange mir,
   Dass williger mein Herz, vom süssen
    Spiele gesättiget, dam mir sterbe.

Die Seele, der im Leben ihr göttlich Recht
Nicht ward, sie ruht auch drunten im Orkus nicht;
   Doch ist mir einst das Heil'ge, das am
    Herzen mir liegt, das Gedicht, gelungen:

Willkommen dannn, o Stille der Schattenwelt!
Zufrieden bin ich, wenn auch mein Saitenspiel
   Mich nicht hinabgeleitet; einmal
    Lebt' ich, wie Götter, und mehr bedarf's nicht.

To the Fates

Grant me just one summer, you mighty ones,
And one autumn, to ripen my song,
  So that my heart, sated with music,
    More willingly will let me die.

The soul, denied in life what was its due
From heaven, rests not even down in Orcus;
  Yet if ever that sacred burden of my heart,
    My poetry, is delivered,

Then welcome, silent world of shadows!
Content I am, even if my song
  Does not descend with me; for once I lived
    As do the gods, and I need no more.

HYPERIONS SCHICKSALSLIED

Ihr wandelt droben im Licht
  Auf weichem Boden, selige Genien!
    Glänzende Götterlüfte
      Rühren euch leicht,
        Wie die Finger der Künstlerin
          Heilige Saiten.

Schicksallos, wie der schlafende
  Säugling, atmen die Himmlischen;
    Keusch bewahrt
      In bescheidener Knospe
        Blühet ewig
          Ihnen der Geist,
            Und die seligen Augen
              Blicken in stiller
                Ewiger Klarheit.

Doch uns ist gegeben
  Auf keiner Stätte zu ruhn,
    Es schwinden, es fallen
      Die leidenden Menschen
        Blindlings von einer
          Stunde zur andern,
            Wie Wasser von Klippe
              Zu Klippe geworfen,
                Jahrlang ins Ungewisse hinab.

HYPERION'S SONG OF FATE

Up there in the light you walk
  On soft ground, blessed spirits!
    The glittering air of the gods
     Caresses you gently
      As the fingers of the harpist
       Touch holy strings.

Free of fate, like sleeping
  Infants breathe those in heaven;
   Chastely protected
   In modest buds,
    Their spirits bloom
     Eternally,
      And their blessed eyes
      Gaze with still
      Eternal clarity.

But to us is given
  No place to rest;
   Suffering humanity
   Dwindles, falls
    Blindly from one
    Hour to the next,
     Like water from cliff
     To cliff cast down
      For years into the unknown.

꒰ꦿ

10

HEINRICH VON KLEIST
(1777–1811)

Kleist is best known for his dramas (especially the comedy *The Broken Jug*, 1812), and for his fiction (e.g., *The Marquise of O.*, 1806, and *Michael Kohlhaas*, 1808). A restless spirit, he supported himself by teaching Greek and by journalistic writing. He killed himself in a suicide pact with a woman he knew only slightly. The essay "On the Marionette Theater" (1810) exemplifies his economical style and is a penetrating analysis of the new self-consciousness characteristic of Romanticism.

On the Marionette Theater

In one of the public gardens of M., where I spent the winter of 1801, I happened one evening to meet Mr. C., who had recently become the first dancer of the Opera and had found extraordinary favor with the public.

I told him that I was amazed to have seen him more than once in a marionette theater which had been stuck up in the market place and was amusing the common people with little farces interspersed with song and dance. He assured me that the pantomime of these puppets gave him much pleasure, and indicated in no uncertain terms that a dancer wishing to improve himself might learn much from them.

Because of the way he had expressed it, his remark seemed more to me than just a random thought, and so I took a seat beside him, wanting to know what his reasons might be for making such an extraordinary assertion.

He asked me if I had not in fact found the movements of the puppets, especially the smaller ones, to be undeniably graceful in their dance.

I could not deny it. A group of four peasants, that danced to the fast rhythm of a rondo, could not have been painted more beautifully by Teniers.

I enquired about the mechanism of these puppets, wanting to know how it was possible to move their individual limbs and joints according to the rhythm of the movement or dance without tangling the fingers in a myriad of strings.

He answered that I should not imagine the puppeteer pulling and posing every limb individually during the successive moments of the dance.

Each movement, he said, has a center of gravity; it is enough to direct this within the puppet, and the limbs, nothing more than pendulums, will follow mechanically of their own accord.

He added that this movement is very simple: moving the center of gravity through a straight line already causes the limbs to describe curves; and often some purely accidental disturbance would set the whole body into a sort of rhythmic motion, similar to dance. I thought this remark began to shed a little light on the enjoyment he claimed to have found in the marionette theater. But I never would have guessed what conclusions he was going to develop from this beginning.

I asked if he believed the puppeteer would have to be a dancer himself, or would at least need to have some concept of what is beautiful in the dance.

He answered that just because a thing is mechanically easy, it does not follow that it can be done without any sensitivity whatsoever.

The line which the center of gravity had to describe was indeed very simple, and, he thought, in most cases straight. In those instances in which it is curved, the law governing its curvature is of the first, or at the outside, of the second order, and even in the latter case it is only elliptical, which is also the most natural form of movement for the extremities of the human body (because of the joints), and therefore requires no great artistry on the part of the puppeteer.

But from another point of view, this line is very mysterious. For it is the path of the dancer's soul; and he doubted that it could be found in any other way than by the puppeteer's putting himself into the puppet's center of gravity—in other words, he must *dance*.

I replied that this work had been described to me as something rather mindless, like the turning of a crank to play a barrel organ.

Not at all, he answered. On the contrary, the movements of his fingers are related to the movement of the puppets fastened to them quite artfully, rather like numbers to their logarithms or the asymptote to a hyperbola. But he believed that even this last infringement of the mind which he had mentioned could be removed, and that their dance could be transferred entirely into the realm of mechanical forces and be produced, as I had imagined, by means of a crank.

I expressed my surprise at seeing him honor this form of entertainment, invented for the common masses, with a devotion usually reserved for the fine arts. Not only did he think it capable of higher development, he seemed actively involved with it himself.

He smiled and said that he would venture to say that if a craftsman would build a marionette according to the specifications he intended to make, he could stage a dance with it which neither he nor any other skillful dancer of his time, not even Vestris, could equal. Have you heard, he asked, since I was silently looking at the ground, have you heard of those mechanical legs which English craftsmen make for those who have unfortunately lost their own?

I said no, I had never seen anything of the sort. I am sorry, he answered, for I am almost afraid that if I tell you these unhappy people can dance with them you will not believe me—What am I saying—they dance? The range of their movements is indeed limited, but those within their command are performed with such ease, calm and grace that any thoughtful man would be amazed.

I said jokingly that he had then indeed found his man. For the craftsman who could build such legs could without question put together a whole marionette according to his specifications.

And what, I asked—for he in turn looked down at the ground a bit self-consciously—what is the nature of these specifications which you would demand of such a man's skill? Nothing, he answered, that we don't already find here: proportion, movability, lightness—only everything to a higher degree; and especially a natural arrangement of the centers of gravity.

And the advantage such a puppet would have over a living dancer?

The advantage? First a negative one, my dear friend, namely this: that it would never put on airs. For putting on airs, as you know, occurs when the soul (vis motrix) lodges in some other point than the center of gravity of the movement. Since the puppeteer has perforce no other point but this in his power by means of the wire or string: all other limbs are what they should be, dead, mere pendulums, following only the law of gravity; an excellent attribute which one looks for in vain in the majority of our dancers.

Just look at P., he continued; when she plays Daphne and, pursued by Apollo, looks back, her soul is sitting in the vertebrae of her spine; she bends as if she would break, like a Naiad of Bernini's school. Look at young F.—when he is standing among the three goddesses as Paris and awards the apple to Venus: his soul (what a horror to watch) sits in his elbow....

Such misjudgments, he added, breaking off, are inevitable, since we have eaten of the fruit of the tree of knowledge. Paradise is locked up, the Cherub is behind us; we must travel around the world and see if there isn't a back door open somewhere.

I laughed—of course, I thought, the mind cannot err where it doesn't exist. But I noticed that he still had more to say, and I asked him to continue. Furthermore, he said, these puppets have the advantage of being antigravitational; they know nothing of the inertia of matter, of all qualities the most antagonistic to dance, because the power lifting them into the air is greater than that fettering them to the earth. What would our dear G. give to be sixty pounds lighter, or to have an equivalent force come to help her with her entrechats and pirouettes? Puppets need the ground only as elves do: to brush against it, and with that momentary restraint to give new life to the swing of the limbs; we need it to rest on it and to recuperate from the exertion of the dance, a moment which is clearly not itself dance and with which we can do nothing except try to make it disappear as much as possible.

I said that as skillfully as he might contrive his paradoxes, he could never make me believe that a mechanical manikin could manifest more loveliness than is inherent in the structure of the human body.

He replied that in this it was manifestly impossible for a human being even to equal the manikin. Only a god could match himself with inanimate matter in this field; this was the point, he said, where the two ends of the ring-shaped world joined one another.

I was more and more amazed: I didn't know what to say to such extraordinary assertions.

It would seem, he continued, taking a pinch of snuff, that I had not read the third chapter of the first book of Genesis attentively enough; and to anyone who did not know about the first period of human development it was impossible to speak intelligently about the following and certainly not about the last.

I said I knew very well what kind of disorder knowledge causes in the natural grace of man. A young man of my acquaintance, I continued, had because of a mere remark lost his innocence before my very eyes as it were, and afterwards had not been able to regain Paradise in spite of all possible efforts.—But, I added, what conclusion can you draw from this?

He asked me what kind of an incident I was speaking of?

About three years ago, I began, I was swimming with a young man who was possessed of a special kind of grace. He might have been sixteen years old, and the first traces of vanity brought on by the favor of women were just beginning to appear. In Paris, not long before this, we both had happened to see the "Youth Pulling a Splinter from His Foot"; the copy of this statue is well known and can be found in most German collections. A glance into a large mirror at the moment he was setting his foot on a stool to dry reminded him of the statue; he smiled and told me of his discovery. Indeed, I had made the same one, but be it to test the security of his native grace or to deal somewhat correctively with his vanity, I laughed and said he must be seeing ghosts. He blushed, and to show me, he lifted his foot a second time; but as one might have easily predicted, the attempt failed. Confused, he lifted his foot a third and fourth and probably a tenth time in vain! He could not produce the same movement again—indeed, the movements which he did make had something so ludicrous about them that I found it difficult to suppress my laughter:—

From this day on, indeed from this moment on, a subtle change could be seen to take place in this young man. He began to stand in front of the mirror for days; and one charm after another left him, an invisible and incomprehensible power seemed to close like an iron net around the free play of his gestures, and within a year's time no trace of that beauty was left which had given such pleasure to those who sought his company. I could look up this very day someone who was witness to that extraordinary and unfortunate incident and who could verify the story as I told it, word for word.

This gives me the opportunity, said Mr. C. with a friendly smile, to tell you another story and you will see right away why it belongs here. While I was traveling to Russia, I spent some time at the estate of Lord G., a Lithuanian nobleman whose sons were practicing their swordsmanship seriously at that time. Especially the older one: he had just returned from the University and, playing the virtuoso, he offered me a rapier one morning when I was visiting his apartment. We fought, but I happened to be his superior; passion came into play, confusing him; almost every one of my thrusts found its mark, and in the end his rapier landed in the corner. Picking up his rapier he said half angrily and half in jest that he had found his master:

but that everyone sooner or later found his and he would soon introduce me to mine. The brothers broke into laughter and exclaimed, come on, come to the wood stall! With that they took me by the hand and led me to a bear which Lord G. was raising in his stables.

As I stepped before him, the bear was standing on his hind legs, his back leaning against the post to which he was chained; his right paw was lifted ready to strike, and he looked into my eyes: this was his fencing position.

I hardly knew whether I was dreaming or not to see myself confronted by such an adversary. Go on, attack, said Lord G., see if you can get to him! When I had recovered from my amazement, I fell to it with my rapier; the bear moved his paw a little and parried the thrust. I tried to seduce him with various feints; the bear remained motionless. Again I attacked with speed and skill, I could not have missed a man's chest; the bear made an imperceptible motion with his paw and parried the thrust. I was now almost in the position of the young Lord G . ... the seriousness of the bear helped to rob me of my composure. Thrusts and feints followed one another, I was drenched with sweat—in vain! The bear not only parried all thrusts like the world's fencing champion; he ignored all feints (something that no fencer in the world could imitate). He stood eye-to-eye with me as if he could read my soul in them, his paw ready to strike, and when my attack was not intended seriously, he did not move.

Do you believe my story?

Absolutely, I exclaimed with delighted applause; it is so right and fitting. I would believe it coming from any stranger—how much more so from you!

Now my good friend, said Mr. C., you know everything you need to understand me. In the natural world we see grace becoming proportionately stronger and more splendid as reflection becomes dimmer and weaker. But just as the intersection of two lines on one side of a point is suddenly found on the other after going through infinity, or as the image in a concave mirror suddenly appears right in front of us again after going far away and finally through infinity: so grace will be found again when knowledge has passed through the infinite in a manner of speaking; so that it appears in its purest form in that human frame which has either no consciousness at all or whose consciousness is infinite, in other words, an automaton or a god.

It seems, I said, somewhat dazed, that we must eat of the fruit of the tree of knowledge again so that we can fall back into the state of innocence?

Yes, he said; that is the last chapter of the history of the world.

11

JOSEPH VON EICHENDORFF
(1788–1857)

An active Catholic, Eichendorff often conveys his devout beliefs through his works. He wrote in almost every genre, but is best remembered for his charming narratives "Memoirs of a Good-for-Nothing" and "The Marble Statue" (both 1826), and for his musical, folk-song-like lyric poems like "The Two Friends" and "The Hermit."

DIE ZWEI GESELLEN

Es zogen zwei rüst'ge Gesellen
Zum erstenmal von Haus,
So jubelnd recht in die hellen,
Klingenden, singenden Wellen
Des vollen Frühlings hinaus.

Die strebten nach hohen Dingen,
Die wollten, trotz Lust und Schmerz,
Was Rechts in der Welt vollbringen,
Und wem sie vorübergingen,
Dem lachten Sinnen und Herz.—

Der erste, der fand ein Liebchen,
Die Schwieger kauft' Hof und Haus;
Der wiegte gar bald ein Bübchen,
Und sah aus heimlichem Stübchen
Behaglich ins Feld hinaus.

Dem zweiten sangen und logen
Die tausend Stimmen im Grund,
Verlockend' Sirenen, und zogen
Ihn in der buhlenden Wogen
Farbig klingenden Schlund.

Und wie er auftaucht vom Schlunde,
Da war er müde und alt,
Sein Schifflein das lag im Grunde,
So still war's rings in der Runde,
Und über die Wasser weht's kalt.

THE TWO FRIENDS

Two sturdy friends set out one day,
Their first time far from home;
Their spirits kindled in delight
So surging, ringing, swirling, singing
The brimming springtime shone.

They set their sights on lofty things
And aimed, through joy and sadness,
To accomplish something fine in life;
And the mind and heart of everyone
They met would laugh with gladness.

The first one found a dear little wife,
Her folks bought them a farm.
He was rocking a baby soon enough
And looking, content, across his fields
From his parlor, snug and warm.

To the second, a thousand voices sang
And lied and tried to draw
Him down to the depths with Siren voice,
And he sunk in the gaudy, ringing surge
Of that voluptuous maw.

And when from the maw he at last emerged
Then he was tired and old;
His little boat was on the rocks,
Such a stillness lay all round about,
And the wind from the water blew cold.

Es singen und klingen die Wellen
Des Frühlings wohl über mir:
Und seh' ich so kecke Gesellen,
Die Tränen im Auge mir schwellen—
Ach Gott, führ uns liebreich zu dir!

DER EINSIEDLER

Komm, Trost der Welt, du stille Nacht!
Wie steigst du von den Bergen sacht,
Die Lüfte alle schlafen,
Ein Schiffer nur noch, wandermüd,
Singt übers Meer sein Abendlied
Zu Gottes Lob im Hafen.

Die Jahre wie die Wolken gehn
Und lassen mich hier einsam stehn,
Die Welt hat mich vergessen,
Da tratst du wunderbar zu mir
Wenn ich beim Waldesrauschen hier
Gedankenvoll gesessen.

0 Trost der Welt, du stille Nacht!
Der Tag hat mich so müd gemacht,
Das weite Meer schon dunkelt,
Lass ausruhn mich von Lust und Not,
Bis dass das ew'ge Morgenrot
Den stillen Wald durchfunkelt.

The surging, ringing, swirling, singing
Of that spring comes back to me;
And when I see such bold young friends
The tears brim over in my eyes—
Oh God, lead us loving to thee!

THE HERMIT

Come, balm of the world, you quiet night!
How softly you climb down the hills;
The breezes all are sleeping;
A single sailor, voyage-weary,
Sings his evening praise to God
From port across the sea.

The years have hurried past like clouds,
And left me here behind, alone,
Forgotten by the world.
Then wonderfully you came to me
As I sat buried in my thoughts
Here in the murmuring woods.

0 quiet night, balm of the world!
I am so weary of the day;
The sea already darkens,
Now let me rest from joy and grief
Till through the quiet woods I see
The eternal sunrise kindle.

12

CLEMENS BRENTANO
(1778–1842)

Best known for the collection of folk songs, *The Boy's Magic Horn* (1806–8), which he published in collaboration with his friend Achim von Arnim (1781–1831), Brentano also wrote fiction, especially fairy tales, and graceful lyrics such as those represented here, which show the influence of folk songs.

ABENDSTANDCHEN

Hör', es klagt die Flöte wieder
Und die kühlen Brunnen rauschen,
Golden weh'n die Töne nieder;
Stille, stille, lass' uns lauschen!

Holdes Bitten, mild Verlangen,
Wie es süss zum Herzen spricht!
Durch die Nacht, die reich umfagen,
Blickt zu mir der Töne Licht.

Evening Serenade

Hark, the flute again lamenting,
As the cool, dim brooklets whisper;
Golden, the notes waft down to us;
Softly, softly—let us listen.

Lovely pleading, gentle yearning,
Sweetly speaking to the heart—
Through the night that folds about me
Glance the beams of music's light.

DER SPINNERIN LIED

Es sang vor langen Jahren
Wohl auch die Nachtigall,
Das war wohl süsser Schall,
Da wir zusammen waren.

Ich sing und kann nicht weinen
Und spinne so allein
Den Faden klar und rein,
Solang der Mond wird scheinen.

Da wir zusammen waren,
Da sang die Nachtigall,
Nun mahnet mich ihr Schall,
Dass du von mir gefahren.

So oft der Mond mag scheinen,
Gedenk ich dein allein,
Mein Herz ist klar und rein,
Gott wolle uns vereinen!

Seit du von mir gefahren,
Singt stets die Nachtigall,
Ich denk bei ihrem Schall,
Wie wir zusammen waren.

Gott wolle uns vereinen,
Hier spinn ich so allein,
Der Mond scheint klar und rein,
Ich sing und möchte weinen!

THE SPINSTRESS'S SONG

Just so, for ages past,
Has sung the nightingale;
How sweetly rang its call
When you were with me last.

I sing to keep from crying
And spin alone tonight
The thread so pure and bright
As long as moonlight's shining.

When you were with me last
So sang the nightingale.
It makes me now recall
How far from me you've passed.

Whenever the moon is shining
I think of you all night;
My heart is pure and bright;
God grant our reuniting.

Since far from me you've passed
Still sings the nightingale
And still its notes recall
When you were with me last.

God grant our reuniting!
I spin alone tonight;
The moon shines pure and bright;
I sing, but would be crying.

13

HEINRICH HEINE
(1797–1856)

Most famous for the deceptively simple-seeming lyrics such as the half-dozen represented here (volumes of poems came out in 1822, 1827, 1844, and 1851), Heine also wrote extensive criticism, travel essays, and miscellaneous journalism. The sardonic wit evident in "The Romantic School" is characteristic of much of his work. Of Jewish descent, Heine adopted Christianity at the age of 28. He lived in Paris for the last 25 years of his life, but always maintained a strong love for his native Germany.

DIE LORELEI

Ich weiss nicht, was soll es bedeuten,
Dass ich so traurig bin,
Ein Märchen aus alten Zeiten,
Das kommt mir nicht aus dem Sinn.

Die Luft ist kühl und es dunkelt,
Und ruhig fliesst der Rhein;
Der Gipfel des Berges funkelt
Im Abendsonnenschein,

Die schönste Jungfrau sitzet
Dort oben wunderbar,
Ihr goldnes Geschmeide blitzet,
Sie kämmt ihr goldnes Haar.

Sie kämmt es mir goldenem Kamme,
Und singt ein Lied dabei;
Das hat eine wundersame,
Gewaltige Melodei.

Den Schiffer im kleinen Schiffe
Ergreift es mit wildem Weh;
Er schaut nicht die Felsenriffe
Er schaut nur hinauf in die Höh',

Ich glaube, die Wellen verschlingen
Am Ende Schiffer und Kahn;
Und das hat mit ihrem Singen
Die Lorelei getan.

THE LORELEI

I can't understand the reason
That I should be so sad;
A strange old fairy story,
I can't put out of my head.

The air is cool, it is twilight,
And peacefully flows the Rhine,
The tops of the mountains glimmer
In the light of the setting sun.

The most beautiful maiden is sitting
Quite wonderfully up there,
Her golden bangles glitter,
She is combing her golden hair.

With a golden comb she combs it,
And all the while sings a song;
Its melody has a power
Mysterious and strong.

The boatman in his shallop
Is seized with a strange, wild grief;
He can only look up to the mountain,
He does not see the reef.

Boat and boatman, I think, were swallowed
At last by the swirling foam;
And that is what the singing
Of the Lorelei has done.

Du bist wie eine Blume

Du bist wie eine Blume
So hold und schön und rein;
Ich schau' dich an, und Wehmut
Schleicht mir ins Herz hinein.
Mir ist, als ob ich die Hände
Aufs Haupt dir legen sollt',
Betend, dass Gott dich erhalte
So rein und schön und hold.

Es ragt ins Meer der Runenstein

Es ragt ins Meer der Runenstein,
Da sitz' ich mit meinen Träumen.
Es pfeift der Wind, die Möwen schrein,
Die Wellen, die wandern und schäumen.

Ich habe geliebt manch schönes Kind
Und manchen guten Gesellen—
Wo sind sie hin? Es pfeift der Wind,
Es schäumen und wandern die Wellen.

You Are Like a Flower

You are like a flower
So fair and pure and fine;
I look at you, and sadness
Steals through this heart of mine.
I feel as if I ought to lay
My hands upon your hair,
Praying that God will keep you
So fine and pure and fair.

The Rune Stone

The rune stone juts into the sea
And I sit there and dream;
Waves roll and foam, the wind blows free,
And seagulls scream.

I have loved many a pretty child
And many a stalwart friend;
Where are they now? Waves toss and foam,
And ever blows the wind.

EIN FICHTENBAUM

Ein Fichtenbaum steht einsam
Im Norden auf kahler Höh.
Ihn schläfert; mit weisser Decke
Umhüllen ihn Eis und Schnee.

Er träumt von einer Palme,
Die fern im Morgenland
Einsam und schweigend trauert
Auf brennender Felsenwand.

CHILDE HAROLD

Eine starke, schwarze Barke
Segelt trauervoll dahin.
Die vermummten und verstummten
Leichenhüter sitzen drin.

Toter Dichter, stille liegt er,
Mit entblösstem Angesicht;
Seine blauen Augen schauen
Inmer noch zum Himmelslicht.

Aus der Tiefe klingt's, als riefe
Eine kranke Nixenbraut,
Und die Wellen, sie zerschellen
An dem Kahn wie Klagelaut.

A Fir Tree

A fir tree stands alone
On a barren Northern height.
It dozes; ice and snowflakes
Envelop it with white.

It's dreaming of a palm tree
That, silent and alone,
Far to the east is grieving
On its burning cliff of stone.

Childe Harold

A stout black bark approaches,
Its sails in gloomy trim;
The mourners sitting in it
Are muffled, mute, and grim.

Dead poet, face uncovered—
Motionless he lies;
And steadily toward heaven's light
Are turned his still blue eyes.

The deep cries out as if
A mermaid shrieked in pain;
Waves dash against the skiff
Like a mighty mourners' train.

DIE LOTOSBLUME

Die Lotosblume ängstigt
Sich vor der Sonne Pracht,
Und mit gesenktem Haupte
Erwartet sie träumend die Nacht.

Der Mond, der ist ihr Buhle,
Er weckt sie mit seinem Licht,
Und ihm entschleiert sie freundlich
Ihr frommes Blumengesicht.

Sie blüht und glüht und leuchtet
Und starret stumm in die Höh';
Sie duftet und weinet und zittert
Vor Liebe und Liebesweh.

The Lotus Flower

The lotus flower trembles
At the sun's majestic light;
She hangs her head and, dreaming,
Awaits the gentle night.

The moon, her lover, wakens her
With softly glowing grace,
And, friendly, she unveils to him
Her pure, sweet flower face.

She shines and burns and blossoms,
Her mute gaze fixed above;
Fragrant, she weeps and trembles
With the joy and pain of love.

FROM THE ROMANTIC SCHOOL
(1836)

Madame de Staël's book *De l'Allemagne* is the only comprehensive source of information on Germany's intellectual life available to the French. And yet, a long time has passed since the appearance of this book and a whole new literature has sprung up in Germany in the meantime. Is it merely a transitional literature? Has it reached or even passed its peak yet? Opinions are divided on this issue. Most people believe that in Germany a new literary period begins with Goethe's death, that the old Germany was carried to the grave along with him; and that the aristocratic era of literature has given way to a democratic one, or, as recently expressed by a French journalist: "the spirit of the individual has ceased, the spirit of the masses has begun."

As for me, I do not feel equipped to judge in such decisive manner about the future evolution of the German spirit. I have, however, been predicting for many years the termination of the "Goethean art period," as I first named this epoch. This prophecy was easy enough! I knew very well the ways and means of those discontented minds, eager to put an end to Goethe's reign over the arts. Even I have been numbered among those insurrectionists against Goethe. Now that Goethe is dead I am seized by a wondrous grief.

Although I am announcing these writings as something of a continuation of Madame de Staël's *De l'Allemagne,* I must, even while praising the information it presents, advise using her book with caution and label it as the work of a coterie from start to finish. Mme. de Staël—glory be to her memory—here opened a kind of salon in book form in which she received German writers and gave them the opportunity of introducing themselves to the civilized public of France. But from the din of multitudinous voices screaming forth from this book, Mr. A. W. Schlegel's fine treble consistently stands out most clearly. Where she is all herself, where the generous, sensitive woman speaks her own with all of her shining heart, with all of the fireworks of her mind's rockets and her brilliant wit: here the book is good, even excellent. But wherever she listens to outside gossip, wherever she tries to follow a certain school whose nature is totally alien and incomprehensible to her, wherever she furthers certain ultramontane tendencies in direct contrast to her Protestant clarity: that is where her book is pathetic and indigestible. Added to this is the fact that she plays favorites not only unconsciously but also in a conscious manner: by singing the praise of Germany's intellectual life, of its idealism, she is actually trying to cast aspersions on France's realism and the material splendor of the Empire. In this respect, her *De l'Allemagne* is similar to the *Germania* of Tacitus, who perhaps wanted to write an indirect satire upon his fellow Romans through his apologia for the Germans.

The school I mentioned above, the one courted and supported by Mme. de Staël, is the Romantic School. That this name pertained to two entirely different phenomena in Germany and in France, will become apparent in the following treatise.

What then was the Romantic School in Germany? It was nothing other than the reawakening of the poetic spirit of the middle ages as it had manifested itself in the songs, paintings and buildings, art and life of that era. This spirit, however, had its origins in Christianity; it was a passion flower sprung forth from the blood of Christ. I do not know if the melancholy flower called passion flower in Germany also bears this name in France, or if folklore attributes to it the same mystic origin. In the chalice of that oddly colored flower, the torturing instruments used for Christ's crucifixion— hammer, pliers, nails, etc.—are clearly pictured. This flower is not at all ugly though, just unearthly, its sight even invoking a sort of horrible delight in our soul like the sharp sweetness one sometimes feels in pain itself. In this respect, the flower would be the most fitting symbol of Christianity itself, whose most horrible attraction lies in the voluptuousness of pain.

Although in France the term Christianity comprises Roman Catholicism only, I do want to point out that I am speaking of the latter exclusively. I speak of that religion in which the first dogmas contain a damnation of the flesh; which not only concedes a superiority of the spirit over the body but also wants to deaden the body in order to glorify the spirit; I speak of that religion through whose unnatural requirements sin and hypocrisy were initially brought into the world; by condemning the flesh the most innocent sensual pleasures were made sin, and hypocrisy had to develop since it was impossible to be all spirit. I speak of that religion which has also become the most dependable pillar of despotism through its dogma which preaches the rejection of all material wealth and instead imposes on its believers the humility of dogs and the patience of angels. People have now recognized the nature of this religion; they are no longer satisfied with references to future heavenly rights; they know that material things have their good side too and are not entirely of the devil, and they vindicate the pleasures of the earth, this beautiful garden of God, our most inalienable heritage. It is because we comprehend so fully all the consequences of that absolute spiritualism, that we may be right in believing in the imminent end of the Christian Catholic ideology. For each era is like a Sphinx, throwing herself into the abyss as soon as her riddle has been solved.

We are far from denying, however, the benevolent influence of the Christian Catholic ideology upon Europe. It was necessary as a healthy reaction against the horribly colossal materialism that had developed within the Roman Empire and which threatened to destroy all of humanity's spiritual beauty. Just as the obscene memoirs of the last century serve somewhat as the *pièces justificatives* of the French Revolution, just as the terrorism of the Committee for the Commonwealth appears as necessary medicine after having read the testimonials of the French nobility since the regency period: thus one recognizes the healing powers of ascetic spiritualism upon reading, say, Petronius' or Apuleius' books, which can well be considered as *pièces justificatives* for Christianity. The flesh had become so arrogant in the Roman world that Christian discipline was necessary to chastise it. After the banquet of a Trimalkio, a fast such as that offered by Christianity was called for. Or perhaps, just as old debauchees excite their sagging flesh to new capacities for sensual pleasures, by whipping themselves: did the aging Rome long for a monk's flogging to find decadent delight in torture itself—voluptuousness in pain?

Terrible over-excitement! It robbed the Roman nation of its last strength. Rome did not collapse of the division into two empires; it was consumed by the same Judaic spirituality on the Bosphorus as on the Tiber, and here as there, Roman history became a slow process of dying, an agony that was to last for centuries. Did perhaps the murdered Judea—by bequeathing its spirituality to the Romans—take revenge upon the victorious enemy like that dying Centaur who so cunningly delivered to Jupiter's son the fatal gown poisoned by his own blood?

Truly, Rome, the Hercules of nations, was consumed by the Judaic poison so effectively that helmet and armor sank from its withered limbs and his imperious battle cry was reduced to the prayers of whimpering priests and trilling castrati.

But that which exhausts the old man strengthens the young one. That spirituality had a positive effect upon the overly robust nations of the North; those more than full-blooded barbaric bodies were spiritualized by Christianity; it was the beginning of European civilization. This is a praiseworthy, saintly side of Christianity. In this respect, the Catholic church deserves our highest admiration and praise. It was able to tame the bestiality of Northern barbarians and to overcome the brutal materialism through its great, ingenious institutions.

The medieval works of art show that domination of matter by spirit and that, in fact, very often is their whole message. The epic writings of that time could easily be classified according to the degree in which this domination occurs.

There can be no mention of lyrical or dramatic poems here; the latter do not exist and the former are similar to each other in all periods like the nightingale's songs each spring.

Although the epic works of the Middle Ages were divided into the sacred and the profane, both genres were thoroughly Christian by nature. Of course, sacred works of art dealt with the Jewish nation exclusively, since it alone was considered sacred and its history, which alone was called sacred, covered the heroes of the Old and the New Testament, the legends— in short the Church. And yet, the profane writings mirror quite well the life in those times with all its Christian aspects and ideas. . . .

As to nonreligious literature, following the categories mentioned above, there is first of all the cycle of Nibelungen and Hero legends; it is still dominated absolutely by pre-Christian thoughts and feelings; here brute force has not yet been moderated into knightly elegance; here they stand like stone monuments, the rigid champions of the North, and the soft light and cultured aura of Christianity does not yet penetrate their iron armor. But the dawn is slowly coming in the old Teutonic forests, the old heathen oaks are being cut down and the clearing becomes an arena where Christ fights the heathen: this is obvious in the epics dealing with Charlemagne which really mirror the crusades, with their religious tendency. From the impact created by Christian spiritualization, developed that strangest phenomenon of the Middle Ages, chivalry, which finally became sublimated into a spiritual knighthood. Worldly knighthood we see most charmingly glorified in the romances about King Arthur, where the sweetest gallantry, the most sophisticated courtesy, and the most adventuresome combativeness reign. . . . Related and interwoven into these romances is the story of the Holy Grail, which glorifies spiritual knighthood. Here we stand confronted by the three most splendid poems of the Middle Ages, the *Titurel,* the *Parcival* and the *Lohengrin.* Here we virtually stand face to face with Romantic poetry itself, we look deep into its large, suffering eyes, and before we know what has happened, it has drawn us into its scholastic web and pulls us into the mad depths of medieval mysticism.

Finally, to be sure, there are poems from that era not totally entranced by Christian spirituality, and which even balk against this influence— poems where the poet escapes from the chains of abstract Christian virtues and joyfully dives into the pleasurable world of glorified sensuality; and Gottfried von Strassburg, who left us the most significant work of this school, *Tristan and Isolde,* is far from being the worst of this lot. . . . The poetic quality in all of these medieval epic poems is of a character distinctly different from the literary works of the Greeks and Romans. In reference to this difference, we call the former Romantic, the latter Classical literature. These terms are, however, not clearly defined categories and in the past have led to the most unpleasant confusion, which was aggravated by calling the old literature not only classic but plastic as well. This was a special source of misunderstandings, since artists should always shape their thematic material plastically—be it Christian or heathen—clear lines must always be visible, in short: the artist's first consideration should be to create in a plastic manner, in modern Romantic art as well as in the old. And indeed, aren't the figures of Dante's *Divine Comedy* or those in Raphael's paintings as plastic as those of Virgil or those on the walls of Herculaneum? The difference lies in the fact that the plastic figures of antique art are completely identical with what they represent, with the idea the artist wanted to convey, so that Odysseus's wanderings, for example, do not signify anything other than a man's wanderings who was a son of Laertes and husband of Penelope and whose name was Odysseus; and that Bacchus in the Louvre is simply Semele's graceful son, audacious melancholy in his eyes, and holy voluptuousness in his curved soft lips. Not so in Romantic art; here a knight's wanderings have also an esoteric significance; they point perhaps towards life's wanderings in general; the conquered dragon is sin, the almond tree that sends its consoling scent to the faraway hero is Trinity, God the Father, God the Son, and God the Holy Ghost, who are one at the same time, just as the almond's shell, meat and pit make up one and the same fruit. When Homer describes a good piece of armor, then it is nothing but a good armor worth so and so many oxen. But when a medieval monk in his poem describes the Holy Virgin's skirts we can rest assured that he imagines under these skirts just as many different virtues; that a special meaning is hidden under these covers of Mary's immaculate virginity which are being serenaded as almond's blossoms, a very sensible thing, considering that her son is thought of as the almond's meat. That is the nature of medieval poetry, which we call Romantic.

Classical art had to present only the finite, and its figures were identical to the artist's idea. Romantic art had to present or at least hint at the infinite and a lot of spiritual references. It therefore took refuge in a system of traditional symbols or rather in metaphorical representation, just as Christ had tried to elucidate his spiritual ideas by way of all sorts of beautiful parables. That explains the mystic, the enigmatic, the wonderful and the effusive elements of medieval works of art. . . .

14

Eduard Mörike
(1804–1879)

An unpretentious Swabian clergyman, Mörike produced some of the finest lyrics in the language. He also wrote fiction and fictionalized biography, notably *Mozart on the Way to Prague* (1895).

Auf eine Lampe

Noch unverrückt, o schöne Lampe schmückest du,
An leichten Ketten zierlich aufgehangen hier,
Die Decke des nun fast vergessnen Lustgemachs.
Auf deiner weissen Marmorschale, deren Rand
Der Efeukranz von goldengrünem Erz umflicht,
Schlingt fröhlich eine Kinderschar den Ringelreihn.
Wie reizend alles! lachend, und ein sanfter Geist
Des Ernstes doch ergossen um die ganze Form—
Ein Kunstgebild der echten Art. Wer achtet sein?
Was aber schön ist, selig scheint es in ihm selbst.

To a Lamp

Still undisturbed, oh lovely lamp, you can adorn,
Suspended here so gracefully on slender chains,
The ceiling of this near-forgotten festive hall.
Around your pure white marble bowl whose rim
A brazen ivy wreath of golden-green entwines,
A band of merry children dancing weave a ring.
It is all so charming! Laughter—yet a gentle shade
Of seriousness flows over and pervades the form:
A work of art of the truest sort. Yet who notices?
No matter—beauty shines in its own blessedness.

An eine Äolshaarfe

Tu semper urges flebilibus modis
Mysten ademptum: nec tibi Vespero
  Surgente decedunt amores,
    Nec rapidum fugiente Solem.

—Horaz

Angelehnt an die Efeuwand
Dieser alten Terrasse,
Du einer luftgebornen Muse
Geheimnisvolles Saitenspiel,
Fang an,
Fange wieder an
Deine melodische Klage!

Ihr kommet, Winde, fern herüber,
Ach! von des Knaben,
Der mir so lieb war,
Frisch grünendem Hügel.
Und Frühlingsblüten unterweges streifend,
Übersättigt mit Wohlgerüchen,
Wie süss bedrängt ihr dies Herz!
Und säuselt her in die Saiten,
Angezogen von wohllautender Wehmut,
Wachsend im Zug meiner Sehnsucht,
Und hinsterbend wieder.

Aber auf einmal,
Wie der Wind heftiger herstösst,
Ein holder Schrei der Harfe
Wiederholt, mir zu süssem Erschrecken,
Meiner Seele plötzliche Regung;

Und hier—die volle Rose streut, geschüttelt,
All ihre Blätter vor meine Füsse!

To an Aeolian Harp

You are always singing in mournful strains
Of your lost Mystes; and the tale of your love
  Does not cease with the rising of Vesper,
    Nor with his flight before the hurrying sun.

                      —Horace

Resting against the ivied wall
Of this old terrace,
You, mysterious-sounding instrument
Of a breeze-borne Muse,
Begin,
Begin again
Your melodious complaint.

You've come, winds, from far away—
Ah! From the fresh green hill
Of the boy I loved so well.
Caressing spring blossoms as you came,
Drenched with fragrances,
How sweetly you oppress this heart:
Now you murmur in the strings,
Drawn by delicious strains of sadness,
Rising to the measure of my longing,
Then dying down again.

But all at once
As the wind gusts stronger,
A lovelier cry of the Harp
Repeats, to my own sweet panic,
The sudden agitation of my soul.

And here—the full-blown rose, as it is shaken,
Strews all its petals at my feet.

APPENDIX

GERMAN ROMANTIC PHILOSOPHERS

No study of the literature of the Age of Goethe, however cursory, is complete without some attention to the philosophy of the time, with which it is intertwined to an unusual degree. For one thing, there were an unusual number of personal connections. Goethe's acquaintance with Herder in Strassburg, beginning in 1770, was a major influence on the young poet, and hence on the Romantic writers whom he in turn influenced. In the 1790s Goethe helped gain appointments at the University of Jena for Fichte and then Schelling, and later still he encouraged young Schopenhauer. In Jena, Fichte knew members of the Schlegel circle, which included Tieck and Novalis; Schleiermacher and Schelling were even more intimately associated with this group. Schelling, Hegel, and Hölderlin were college friends at Tübingen. Not surprisingly, the philosophy of the time shares certain tendencies with the literature: a distrust of the empirical, rational thought of the Enlightenment; a corresponding attraction to the subjective, intuitive, imaginative, and emotional aspects of humanity; and a striving toward some sort of transcendent unity.

Among earlier philosophers, the Romantics looked back especially to those of a Neoplatonic or mystical cast. Plotinus, Bruno, and the English Platonist Shaftesbury all exerted influences. Schelling, Tieck, Novalis, and others of the Schlegel circle were much taken with the mystical system of Jacob Boehme (1575–1624), who described the natural world as an emanation or degeneration of the divine One into a series of polar tensions—sweetness and bitterness, light and darkness—connected in a "centrum," living fire. And almost all of the writers of this age, Goethe as much as any, felt the impact of Spinoza and his quasi-pantheistic view that subject and object, "intelligence" and "extension" are but aspects of the same substance, God, in which everything has its being.

The towering philosophical figure of the immediately preceding generation was of course Immanuel Kant (1724–1804), himself a product and high point of the Enlightenment, though his critiques undercut the ground of rationalism so drastically that he sometimes seems its enemy. He considered himself in the same tradition as "the illustrious Locke," as he called the English empiricist; his task was to rebuild sounder foundations for philosophy and morals after the demolition of traditional bases by David Hume, who had carried Locke's reasoning to a position of complete skepticism. Locke, Kant explained, investigated "the matter of knowledge [obtained] from the senses," plus the form as it inheres in the knowledge; but the transcendental philosophy deduces, independently of the matter of knowledge, the "*a priori* conditions of the possibility of experience," i.e., the framework of conception before any sensation is involved (*Critique of Pure Reason,* trans. Norman Kemp Smith [London: MacMillan, 1929], hereafter abbreviated *CPR*, pp. 121, 126). The *Critique of Pure Reason,* which first appeared in 1781, gives a rigorous philosophical embodiment to the tendency toward a subjective orientation of reality already in the air in less rigorous form—in Rousseau, for example. Kant's Preface to the second edition shows that he realizes the revolutionary implications of his approach:

> Hitherto it has been assumed that all our knowledge must conform to objects. But all attempts to extend our knowledge of objects by establishing something in regard to them *a priori,* by means of concepts, have, on this assumption, ended in failure. We must therefore make trial whether we may not

have more success in the tasks of metaphysics, if we suppose
that objects must conform to our knowledge. . . . We should
then be proceeding precisely on the lines of Copernicus'
hypothesis. Failing of satisfactory progress in explaining the
movements of heavenly bodies on the supposition that they all
revolved round the spectator, he tried whether he might not
have better success if he made the spectator to revolve and the
stars to remain at rest.

(*CPR*, Preface to Second Edition [1787], p. 22)

Kant defines his "transcendental idealism" as "the doctrine that
appearances are to be regarded as being, one and all, representations only,
not things in themselves, and that time and space are therefore only sensible
forms of our intuitions, not determinations given as existing by themselves,
nor conditions of objects viewed as things in themselves" (*CPR*, p. 345).
Neither space nor time is "an empirical concept which has been derived
from outer experiences"; each is merely a necessary *a priori* representation,
which underlies all outer intuitions (*CPR*, pp. 68, 74–76). In apprehending
reality our minds also impose other *a priori* categories such as quantity,
quality, relation, and modality (*CPR*, p. 113).

Kant's system forever bars us from knowing the ultimate nature of
the thing-in-itself beyond the vehicles of our thought-forms. "Where the
understanding has not previously combined," he says, "it cannot dissolve,
since only as having been combined *by the understanding* can anything that
allows of analysis be given to the faculty of representation" (*CPR*, pp. 82-
83, 152). But Kant is neither a Berkeleian idealist nor a skeptic; the mind,
he says, needs things-in-themselves as its objects, and is conditioned by
them. On the other hand, his basic system is a belief in an underlying "unity
of the world-whole" (Cf. *CPR*, pp. 208-238). An adequate notion of reality
may be attained within the limitations of our thought-forms if these
limitations are carefully charted. Thus in Kant can be seen a resemblance to
two complementary Romantic attitudes. The first is a refinement of Hume's
position—a distrust of the phenomenal world, which is regarded as an
unavoidable "veil" which partially reveals at the same time that it forever
hides the ultimate reality. The second is the more optimistic affirmation of

the human mind as an active force in "half-creating" nature.

Another powerful philosophical predecessor of Romanticism was Johann Gottfried Herder (1744–1803). Raised in the tradition of Pietism— the enthusiastic, evangelical wing of German Protestantism—Herder became a protegé of Kant while a student at Königsberg. Gradually, however, he shifted his philosophical orientation to opposition to this former master. The shift was reinforced by his early acquaintance, which proved to be life-long, with the anti-rationalist critic and thinker Johann Georg Hamann, called "the Magus of the North" (1730–1788). Like Hamann, Herder came to object to the excessively abstract and analytical thinking which he felt was characteristic of Enlightenment philosophy—including that of Kant. He insisted, rather, on the organic wholeness of experience, and believed that thought processes could not be compartmentalized into faculties or abstract functions. Instead, he felt, mental activities are always qualified by historical circumstances, especially language, which is the vehicle of reason. Hence the culture into which one is born is of central importance in the formation of one's character and ideas. Because of his emphasis on the historical development of the cultures of different peoples, Herder became one of the pioneers in the revival of interest in folk materials which stirred the imaginations of Goethe and Schiller in the 1770s, and of the Romantic writers after them. Herder acknowledges the distinctive achievements of humanity in different times and places, and he refrains from judging customs and institutions against any absolute criteria. Along with this cultural relativism, however, he sees a single dynamic energy, the power of nature, fulfilling itself in all possible ways in different creatures and cultures. Though the same principles of reason and justice operate in all people, they may develop different manifestations among the Chinese, Hindus, Phoenicians, and Greeks. This notion of organic development Herder applies not only to past history and the contemporary world, but to the future as well. In his *Ideas for a Philosophy of the History of Mankind* Herder sees a gradual improvement of society in past centuries, and looks forward to continued progress as humanity continues to realize its innate potential.

The end toward which any thing that is not simply a dead instrument progresses, must lie within itself. If we had been created to strive, forever in vain, toward some unattainable external point of perfection, as a magnet turns toward the north, then we might pity not only ourselves, as blind machines, but likewise that Being Who thus condemned us to the fate of Tantalus, because He had formed our race for such a malicious, diabolical spectacle. . . . But fortunately, the nature of things teaches us no such deluded view; considering mankind as we know it, according to the laws intrinsic to it, we find in man nothing higher than humanity itself; for, even if we think of angels or gods, we think of them as nothing more than ideal, higher human beings.

(*Ideas,* Book XV, Chap. 1)

Herder's optimistic belief in progress, and his emphasis on following innate human impulses, rather than externally imposed guides such as rational analysis or abstract codes, struck a responsive chord in the minds of the young writers of Storm and Stress, and in their successors who formulated the attitudes of Romanticism.

Open critics of Kant, like Herder, posed perhaps less of a threat to this system than avowed disciples, like Johann Gottlieb Fichte (1762–1814), who carried subjective orientation far beyond the carefully balanced structure of the *Critique of Pure Reason,* and in thus out–Kanting Kant, articulated a philosophical view highly appealing to the Romantics. The child of poor Saxon peasants, Fichte was helped to an education by a local gentleman who recognized his unusually keen mind. He married a niece of the poet Klopstock; seeking the acquaintance of Kant, whom he had come to admire, he impressed the master so that Kant helped him achieve the deserved reputation that led to his appointment in 1794 as professor at Jena. There, and later in Berlin, Fichte was regarded as a brilliant lecturer and distinguished himself, during these years of Napoleon's rise and triumph, by his ardent German nationalism (seen especially in his *Addresses to the German Nation,* 1807–8).

The importance which Kant attributes to the individual mind is stressed even further by Fichte, who subsumes everything Other under the

"Ich" or *"I."* His system, *Wissenschaftslehre* or Science of Knowledge, develops Kant's idealism by focussing narrowly on the experience of consciousness, in a manner reminiscent of the dynamic polar ontology of Boehme. Fichte teaches "that all reality —*for us*, of course—is produced solely through the imagination." But rather than speaking, as Kant does, of the "deception" of the imagination, he sees in imagination "truth, and the only possible truth." The *"I"* produces all things—all sense objects as well as thoughts—and in so doing it also produces itself. Fichte equates being with consciousness: *"What* was I before I became self-conscious? The obvious answer is, *I* was not at all, for I was not *I*. The *I* exists only in so far as—and in the same way as—it is conscious of itself." Such a question is "improper" in the first place, showing a confusion between subject and object.

Neither *I* nor *not-I* (subject and object) can exist independently of the other; the *I* simultaneously brings itself and the object of its thought into being. Fichte equates his *"I"* and *"not-I"* with Spinoza's *intelligence* and *extension;* but he says that Spinoza's *one substance* (God) is nothing more than another way of speaking of an absolute *I*. The *not-I* is a limitation of the *I*, but this limitation or determination is necessary in order for it to know itself. This limitation may also be expressed as passivity: the *I* is passive in relation to the *not-I,* but it can know itself by this limitation of its own pure activity. The *not I*, since it is produced by the *I*, is thus actually a part of the *I*.

The *I* which joins with the *not-I* in a perception or idea is not the total or absolute *I*; it is only that part of the absolute which comes into being— i.e., into consciousness—by self-limitation. There is an infinite potential in the absolute *I* waiting to be developed and brought into being. The *I* is divisible—able to be "determined" by *not-I*—in an infinite number of ways.

Fichte limits his speculation as to the nature of any ground of being besides the *I*. Like Kant, he sees the possibility of knowledge strictly limited by the nature of the mind. The ultimate ground of reality, he says, is still in a sense within the *I*, though as long as it is beneath the level of consciousness and not controlled by the will, it may also be regarded as foreign and heterogeneous. The *I* and this ultimate ground simultaneously posit each other in "a primal interaction between the *I* and a something outside of itself, of which nothing more can be said than that it must be the complete opposite of the *I*."

At the end of his lectures in 1794 Fichte departed from his strict mathematical proofs in an ebullient praise of the human mind entitled *The Dignity of Man.* This discourse makes clear that in the conscious I the individual self is transcended and all minds merge in one human spirit. It is preeminently through the *I*, he says, that

> order and harmony comes into dead, formless matter. From man alone does *regularity* spread out around him to the limit of his perception; and as he extends this limit farther, so are order and harmony also extended farther. . . . Through [his observation] the heavenly bodies cohere, and become but *one* organized body; through it the suns move in their appointed courses. Through the *I* arises the enormous gradation from the worm to the seraph; in it is the system of the whole spirit-world, and man rightly expects that the law, which he gives to it and to himself, shall be valid for it; rightly expects the imminent universal acknowledgement of his law.

Fichte, like Novalis and many of the English Romantics, envisages the continual perfection of man through mental expansion; physical obstacles are mere petty illusions:

> Break the hut of clay in which he lives! He is in his being absolutely independent of everything that is outside of himself. . . .
>
> Oppose, frustrate his plans! You may delay them; but what are a thousand years or yet more thousands in the year-book of mankind?—no more than a light morning dream on awakening. He lives on and he *acts* on, and that which appears to you as his disappearance is simply an extension of his sphere; what to you seems death, is his ripening for a higher life. In every moment of his existence he tears something new outside of himself into his circle; and he will continue to tear things to himself until he has assimilated everything—until all matter bears the stamp of his influence, and all spirits form One Spirit with his spirit.

Fichte's ringing celebration of the infinite potential of the human spirit is in tune with his time: it perhaps reflects something of the Promethean enthusiasm of the Storm and Stress and of Faust's eternal strivings, and it anticipates the visionary optimism of Romantic writers like Novalis and Shelley, and the tragic aspiration of Hölderlin. It can also be seen in Fichte's younger contemporary, Friedrich Wilhelm Joseph von Schelling (1775-1854), who was an intimate of the Jena circle, and who in fact, in 1803, married Caroline Böhmer Schlegel, whom he first knew as the wife of Auguste Wilhelm Schlegel. Schelling is distinguished in this group by his religious skepticism and his interest in natural science. At first he considered his philosophical writings merely an extension of the *Wissenschaftslehre*, but eventually his thought developed in directions counter to that of Fichte.

Schelling's idealism takes a different orientation from Fichte's. Rather than focussing on the *I*, Schelling insists on a unity of Being, of nature and spirit. "Nature must be visible spirit, spirit invisible nature," he says in *Ideas toward a Philosophy of Nature* (1797). "Thus *here,* in the absolute identity of a spirit *within* us and nature *outside* of us, lies the solution of how an external nature is possible." This unity, he explains elsewhere, extends to the whole cosmos: "The universe, i.e., the infinity of forms in which the eternal interconnection [Band] affirms itself, is only universe, true totality *(totalitas),* by virtue of interconnection, i.e., through unity in multiplicity. Totality thus requires unity *(identitas),* without which it is in no wise conceivable" (*Of the World Soul*).

Schelling believes that the endless variety of phenomena returns to the ultimate ground in unity, from which it has degenerated, through progressively more complex polarities that subsume ever wider diversity within the unity of spirit. In epistemological terms the polarity is between subject (spirit) and object (nature), neither of which can exist without the other, but each of which, like the poles of a magnet, depends on the other for existence. In this view of reality as a dynamic structure of polarities, all based in a pervading unity, we can perhaps see combined influences of Boehme and Spinoza, and also an anticipation of Hegel's dialectic.

Schelling does not limit his theory of polarities to epistemology: he boldly extends his system to chemistry, physics, astronomy, and biology.

He complains—sounding much like Blake complaining of the ratios of Newton—that the natural sciences are superficial in their concern for the mechanical relations of things, without regard for the ultimate ground where spirit and phenomena are one. A good deal of his writing on *Naturphilosophie* is concerned with incorporating such phenomena as light, magnetism, electricity, chemical action, and organic growth into his system, as tangible manifestations of spirit at work in nature. Schelling's friend Heinrich Steffens pursued similar speculations based more directly on laboratory experiments. These were heady times, when not only philosophers, but poets such as Goethe and Novalis, and in England Coleridge and Shelley, felt that all branches of knowledge—experimental science, metaphysics, and poetry—were on the brink of falling together into one grand synthesis, like a puzzle whose key was at last being discovered.

Like Herder, Schelling often regards reality as a vast organism, its parts all connected, and all developing into higher forms, that is, to more extreme and complex polarities, rising from the inorganic to the organic and finally to consciousness. No finite phenomena have absolute existences in themselves; they are always merely stages of development (*Hemmungspunkte*) of the total continuum eternally evolving toward the absolute whence they arose: "Nature *exists* nowhere as product; all isolated products in nature are only appearances, not the absolute product in which absolute energy exhausts itself." Nothing ever merely *is*; everything is always *becoming*.

Human consciousness is the apex of natural development, in which the blind struggle of spirit back to unity breaks through into new wholeness and freedom. At the end of his *System of Transcendental Idealism,* Schelling concludes that man's artistic experience is the supreme form of consciousness. The poetic power, imagination (*Einbildunskraft*), is the highest philosophical faculty, because, like the generative power of nature itself, it creates a complex, unified object by setting up a balanced tension of opposites, of unity in multiplicity. In fact, what we call "nature" is itself merely "a poem that lies inaccessible in a strange, wonderful writing": it is an "Odyssey of the spirit which, wonderfully deluded, in seeking itself flees itself." Artistic creation is at the same time both the highest product of this

Odyssey—the spirit's nearest return to unity of being—and the Rosetta
Stone by which nature's meaning is deciphered.

Friedrich Schleiermacher (1768–1834), a theologian rather than a
systematic philosopher like Fichte or Schelling, embodies in his religious
writings many central attitudes of Romanticism. Raised in the Pietist faith
of the Herrnhüters, he studied at the University of Halle and became
chaplain of the Charity Hospital in Berlin. While there he became acquainted
with the Schlegel circle and contributed pieces to the *Athenaeum*. One of his
earliest and best known works, *On Religion: Addresses to its Cultured
Despisers* (1799), is characteristically deeply felt and intuitive, both in its
method of presentation and in the kind of religion it advocates. Rejecting
Enlightenment analysis, and in tune with the subjective orientation of his
contemporaries, Schleiermacher finds true religion within the sometimes
inexpressible inner convictions of the individual rather than in external
dogmas, ethical precepts, or rational proofs.

> Man is born with the religious capacity, as with every other;
> and if only his sense for the innermost depths of his own being
> is not forcefully suppressed, if only all fellowship between
> himself and the Primal Being is not shut off and blocked—for
> these are certainly the two elements of religion—then infallibly
> it will develop in every person, each after his own fashion. But
> unfortunately that is, to a great extent, just what happens these
> days from childhood on. With pain I daily see how the rage for
> calculation and explanation quite blocks up the mind, and how
> everything conspires to bind people to the finite—and to a
> very small part of it at that—so that the infinite is removed as
> far as possible from their sight. (Third *Address*)

In the *Addresses* Schleiermacher shows an affinity with Spinoza in
his sense of the oneness of all things in God: he defines religion itself as the
inner participation of the individual in the infinite and eternal divine being:

> To be sure, religion is essentially contemplation, and you
> would never call anyone *pious* who goes around impenetrable
> and dullwitted, whose mind is not open to the life of the world.
> But this contemplation is not, like your knowledge of Nature,

concerned with the existence of some finite thing in connection with and in contrast to another finite thing; nor is it even, like your knowledge of God—using here, incidentally, if I may, an old-fashioned expression—concerned with the nature of the first cause, in itself and in relation to all which is both cause and effect. Rather, the contemplation of the pious is simply the immediate consciousness of the universal existence of all finite things in and through the infinite, and of all temporal things in and through the eternal. To seek and find this in all that lives and moves, in all evolution and change, in all doing and suffering—simply to have an immediate conviction of life itself and to know that it is such a universal existence: that is religion. Religion attains peace where it finds this; where this is hidden, there it finds frustration and anxiety, misery and death. And thus it is beyond doubt a life in the infinite nature of the whole, in the One and the All, in God, having and possessing all things in God and God in all things. But it is not knowledge and understanding—neither of the world nor of God: rather it simply recognizes these, without being them. And it is itself an impulse, a revelation of the infinite in the finite—it being seen in God, and God in it. (Second *Address*)

Religious writers of the Enlightenment tended to treat physical nature as a language left behind by a *deus absconditus*—a God withdrawn to a higher realm—whereby the individual mind, through the exercise of reason, could come to know Him. Schleiermacher is characteristically Romantic in regarding nature as a much more immediate revelation of divinity. Critics of English literature call this attitude in Wordsworth his "sacramental vision" of nature; similarly, Novalis in *Christendom or Europe* makes one of the definitive aspects of Christianity "belief in the efficacy of all things of the earth to be the wine and bread of eternal life"; and the brooding landscapes of the painter Kaspar David Friedrich (1774–1840) convey the sense of a supernatural power that is mysteriously *present* in the rocks and sky.

The philosopher of the post–Kantian era who claims the most respect from modern readers is Georg Wilhelm Friedrich Hegel (1770–1831). Though his own system evolved too late to have much influence on the development of Romanticism, his thought in many ways reflects influences and attitudes of the Romantic writers. At the heart of Hegel's system is the process of dialectic, the resemblance of which to Boehme's and Schelling's ideas has already been noted. In Hegel's view, ultimate reality is not to be found in any stable form or substance, but rather in a constant intellectual process of *becoming*. As Frederick Copleston sums it up, "For Hegel the Absolute is not an identity about which nothing further can be said: it is the total process of its [own] self-expression or self-manifestation in and through the finite" (*A History of Philosophy*, VII, Pt. I, p. 206). The mode of this process is dialectical: that is, a conception at a given stage (thesis) evokes its own negation or opposite (antithesis), and the two are resolved in a higher form (synthesis), which in turn becomes the thesis in a new triadic development. A key term for Hegel is *aufheben,* which can mean "to put an end to," "to preserve," or "to lift up"; used dialectically it expresses the simultaneous negation of the thesis in its antithesis, and the preservation of both in their higher synthesis. Hegel's first full-length book, *The Phenomenology of the Spirit* (1807), narrates the development of the human mind (both in the individual and in the history of mankind) in an ever higher *aufhebung*. The first stage of mental development is consciousness, i.e., awareness of objects; the second stage (antithesis) is self-consciousness; and the synthesis, which Hegel calls Reason, is the resolution of both in a yet closer approximation to the All. But this is just the bare outline: the *Phenomenology* is vastly complicated by multiple levels of meaning, irony, and satire. For example, Hegel dramatizes the soul's development into self-consciousness by presenting the two "selves" (perceiving and perceived) as master and slave—a relation which has historical and social, as well as psychological and metaphysical, levels of reference. M. H. Abrams compares *The Phenomenology of the Spirit* to Finnegan's *Wake,* and points out that it is really a *Bildungsbiographie*, the narrative of a soul's development, comparable to Goethe's *Wilhelm Meister*, Novalis' *Heinrich von Ofterdingen*, and Wordsworth's *Prelude*. Another critic, Loewenberg, calls Hegel's dialectic "an application on a grand scale of the histrionic principle involved in romantic irony." Thus Hegel is one more instance of the fact that the philosophy and the imaginative literature of the time reflect many of the same distinctive qualities.

3